Beauty

&

Fiction

by Whickwithy

Beauty & Fiction

All rights reserved

ISBN: 978-1-7348221-0-6

Beauty and Fiction by Whickwithy

First published in Apr 2020

Latest update Aug 2020

I'll stick with my favorite quotes that apply.

"The smell of a world that is burned"
    - Jimi Hendrix

"Power at its most vicious is a riposte to powerlessness."
    - Simone de Beauvoir

"Great minds discuss ideas; average minds discuss events; small minds discuss people."
    - Eleanor Roosevelt

"Sure he (Fred Astaire) was great, but don't forget that Ginger Rogers did everything he did, ...backwards and in high heels."
    - Bob Thaves, "Frank and Ernest" comic strip

"Darkness cannot drive out darkness; only light can do that. Hate cannot drive out hate; only love can do that."
    - Martin Luther King, Jr.

"And nothing natural is evil"
    -Marcus Aurelius

"The unexamined life is not worth living"
"Let him that would move the world first move himself"
"From the deepest desires often come the deadliest hate"
    - Socrates

It is very much like waking from a nightmare to find a dream.

I'd much rather be writing poetry.

Contents

The road foreword

Humanity has been derailed for more than three millennia. It's time to get back on track.

The real story

Long ago, we were little more than an animal with the gifts of heightened awareness and intellect. These gifts have been squandered. We missed a step and never fulfilled the fundamentals of a truly human existence. Our humanity remains to be discovered.

There is one crucial aspect of being human that has never been readily apparent. It is the key without which our humanity remains locked away. For reasons you will begin to understand, we have completely blinded ourselves to its existence for all of these long millennia.

Knowing that something is wrong is not the same as doing something about it. Even admitting the importance and necessity for change can be a challenge. That is the situation as it has existed since earliest mankind.

One subject is *seemingly* complex and very certainly intimidating. The earliest humans were aware that something was wrong. They just failed to admit it. They were an animal that finally had the wit to know something was wrong but at a loss as to what could be done about it. They were baffled. So, they turned out the lights.

A barrier of fear and delusion was erected, behind which the surprising, tremendous potential of our sentience still resides. That barrier conceals our humanity behind a wall of absurdity. We may now exit the Theater of the Absurd.

Surprises

Our current existence is full of surprises as one peers past the nonsensical condition and perceives our sentient state.

Surprise number one is that we thoroughly accept our absurd unruly state, as if it were the best we can do.

Surprise number two is that we put rules and regulations in place that are enforced in order to *limit* our inhumanity, thus making the case that we remain inhuman.

Whickwithy

Surprise number three is that our heightened awareness is not so easily fooled. Deep down inside, we know something is missing, something is wrong. Because we can't admit what is wrong, everything goes awry. This is the only explanation that honour, integrity and a whole host of finer human qualities continue to elude us. The awareness of a gaping hole in our existence causes a ceaseless ache in the human race. We repeatedly reach for but never grasp our humanity.

Surprise number four is that we continue to try to *become* human by mimicking how we know a sentient being should behave. That will never be enough.

Surprise number five is that we already *are* human. We just retain a destructive trait from animals that must be overcome.

Surprise number six is that the transformation into sentience is virtually instantaneous. We have tried to thrash our way out of our less than desirable situation for millennia, believing that it should take long centuries (if ever) to slog our way past the tendencies of a beast. That is the animal prancing around in its newly acquired apparel of heightened awareness and intellect while avoiding the mirror as well as the answer to our dreams. Our nightmares are the result.

We have only been learning to *act* human. What we require is the release of our animal legacy. In other words, by peering without fear or restraint beyond the inhumanity of the animal we can discover what will finally make us human.

We can become a full-fledged sentient race of emotionally balanced, rational, well-adjusted sentient beings now, not at some distant later date.

Surprise number seven is that, amidst all of the seeming complexity and confusion of sentient life, there is only one, rather minor, rather simple, critical change required. With that change, our humanity can flourish.

The nature of the rather simple, required change is surprise number eight. It has remained virtually undetectable due to historical precedents of conditioning, paradigms, and inertia that carry through to the present.

As we first grasped for reason, we embraced unreason. The motivation and justification for this failure were so unlikely that we never saw it coming.

Surprise number nine is that it requires a reorientation of our awareness and intellect first. A tangible change in outlook is required in order to reveal that which will make us human. We can then, finally, take the step that will definitively differentiate us from the beasts.

Accepting that humanity misperceived the situation is a daunting task. It requires overturning millennia of delusion. An intimidating prospect has held us back since the beginning, before we ever crawled out of our caves.

The nonsense that we accepted was first created by humans much closer to a monkey than a sentient being. Bewilderment was brought on by our heightened awareness which was unprepared for what it encountered. We have only embellished the nonsense as our sentient awareness and intellect became more refined. The nonsense always stayed one step ahead of our reason. All because we cringed away from a *seemingly* unsettling realization.

Over a lifetime, we are trained to look away rather than confront that which is required in order to attain our sentience ascendance. Over the millennia, the conditioning becomes more sophisticated in order to avoid that which becomes more obvious every day. Our path diverges farther and farther from something resembling sentience as time progresses and the absurdities multiply.

Getting through three millennia of layer upon layer of conditioning and paradigms is challenging indeed. It took me three manuscripts and more than a decade of effort to finally be able to express it definitively - and that was only after three or four decades in which I kept observing and pondering what the hell was wrong with mankind.

We remain one seriously messed up beast and all because we have avoided one issue for the most ridiculous reason.

The perplexing situation has landed us in a stupour in which we can scarcely discern the difference between human and animal behaviour. Animal behaviour is accepted right alongside human behaviour as if that should be expected.

We must see through the nonsense and boldly face the situation and its implications. Resolution of the dilemma that our ancient ancestors feared down to the core of their being is achieved by just opening our eyes. We can be well on our way to becoming human soon.

Why is it that we continue to return to the same old violent, brainless solutions that never work? Why is it that we act like a dull-witted monkey when facing challenges? Isaac Asimov may have said it best. "Violence is the last refuge of the incompetent." We seem to revel in violence. Of course, I am not talking about just physical violence. That is just the most blatant embodiment of violence. Violence is ever-present in our condition, not our sentient nature. It is a distraction from what really impedes our progress.

What drives the paranoia, so reminiscent of a mindless beast, when confronted with challenges? Even in the best of times, the paranoia lurks in the background. Why do we continue to feel so terribly vulnerable when humanity has conquered everything it has faced? Or, has it?

The biggest surprise for me was realizing how obvious the problem is. There is so much evidence that it is utterly astonishing. Now, everywhere I look I see it as plain as day.

How did we avoid perceiving the primary difference between human and animal? Our brutal, witless, distracted approach towards our situation demands explanation. There is a reason that mankind bashes through life wreaking havoc. That reason is a mirage. Once the mirage is banished, we will no longer remain less than human.

So far, we have only progressed from the state of an animal to the state of a deranged animal. It is like a scale that tipped towards the brute animal in the absence of that which definitively distinguishes human from animal. Our heightened awareness and intellect create a vast sea of confusion in its absence. Without that which allows the finer qualities of humanity to flourish, our intellect and awareness only make us unstable and exceedingly dangerous.

Heightened awareness has given us the potential to identify that which distinguishes human from animal. Our heightened intellect has given us the wit and accumulated knowledge to create the all-important change that can make us human. We need no longer *act* human. We can *be* human.

We have deceived our shared consciousness and it is becoming more restless. No matter how vociferously we attempt to deceive ourselves, our sentient awareness cannot be fooled. At some deep level, we know it is deceit. Our problems and confusion compound as our restless sentience more clearly detects the underlying deceit.

There is something missing. It unhinges our sentient existence. For the sake of our humanity, we must move beyond the bounds of a witless animal and fulfill our sentient state by accepting a defining difference of being human.

History

Millennia ago, we created the basis for mimicking what it means to be human and never looked back. In all ways, it was little more than window dressing. We have been completely terrified to look through the window to see what is really going on. Instead, we dressed it up in fiction. In such a way, we have remained a gibbering beast.

There are so many references that make this apparent that it is startling. We have clearly avoided taking a hard look in the mirror in a desperate attempt to avoid the issue that, ironically, contains our sentient ascendence.

The misery, cruelty, inhumanity, and self-centeredness of the human race today is little different from that which existed many millennia ago. We have put a patina of politeness (often referred to as political correctness) upon the absurdity of it all that brushes off with the slightest wind of change because it is nothing more than window dressing. We shrug and suggest it's just unstable individuals. While, in fact, it is the human condition (not nature) and it is just getting worse. Foolish finger-pointing from all sides never ends and never resolves anything. We create shiny new toys and consider everything alright.

As we first attained our sentience many millennia ago, we expressed the high ideals we sensed, such as honour, integrity, and dignity.   As time progressed, those ideals remained unfulfilled.   We repeatedly failed to attain them. We sense them but cannot attain them.

Those ideals, in their ongoing absence, are becoming accepted as unattainable rather than realizing there is a missing piece of the puzzle. We are becoming frozen into the state of mimicry and despair.

This is one of the greatest mysteries and primary riddles of our existence that drove me on. How could we sense these high ideals, in the first place, if we could never seem to attain them? Something is clearly missing as we flail about.

In their absence, we have begun to surrender to the concept of existentialism and it is accelerating.   We are beginning to accept that we are little more than a very bright, highly destructive animal that can never be more than absurd.

Nowadays, there are those that gladly, loudly, and proudly pontificate regarding their beastliness as the patina on humanity's behaviour continues to fade.   Others just joke about it. Bumbling buffoons populate the world stage (of our Absurdity).   Few hold out hope that higher ideals can be ever attained. We are exhausted from performing on the stage of the Theater of the Absurd.

Our humanity is more than an act played out on a stage of fools.   We need to look in the mirror.   The reason for the ongoing complete absurdity of our situation is revealed.

We have accepted that something is wrong *and* that there is nothing to do about it other than wail, tear our hair out, and wait, hoping it will get better someday. That day has arrived.

Advanced humanity

This is the advanced course in being human. This is about what it really means to be human rather than acting out the part of a human, sentient being.

Attempting to emulate humanity will never be enough. The evidence of our tomfoolery is all around us.   There is something missing. We require the element that is missing from our state of sentience. We need to feel it in our bones.

Breaking the barriers of deceits, delusions, paradigms and conditioning that hold us in thrall is not easily done. I could not have done it myself if I had not spent forty years contemplating our situation seriously, while remaining convinced that our current antics are baseless foolishness.

Anyone can see that it is an absurd existence. Our media and literature are littered with it and we just shake our heads and accept it all as "just the way it is". That's foolishness.

It is another matter entirely to realise *why* the absurd aspects exist and that they have no reason to exist other than the misconceptions we have fed ourselves.

It is first necessary to see through the absurd delusions we have put in place. These obscure the realization of what it will take for humanity to become so much more.

There is a very tangible change to our circumstances that no animal, only a sentient race, could ever identify, much less achieve. We begin the journey towards an emotionally stable, reasoning, sane state by doing so.

What would happen if every individual human felt inherently validated in its existence? How different would humanity be? What if there were no gnawing feeling that something was missing? What if we could clearly see that we are so much more than just a smart, demented animal? What if feelings of self-worth were validated, rather than undermined? What could possibly change us from the gibbering beast we currently portray?

Ever since our ancient ancestors stumbled disastrously, we have avoided the primary conundrum of sentient existence. There is one change that can make us completely human, sentient, and worthy of pondering the concept of sapience.

The ramifications of how everything will change are stunning to contemplate; the vehicle of that change astonishing. The beast can be left behind. To do so, a dichotomy must become uniformity. Ironically, we have stared it right in the face since the very beginning and always turned away in confusion, thus accepting so much less than our humanity.

Self-respect, the inherent validation of our existence, leads to the whole host of human, humane, sentient characteristics. *Everything* regarding humanity is revolutionized by it. Self-respect of the individual is currently being undermined.

I wish I could provide a concise overview of the problem that we face and its resolution but more than three thousand years of delusions makes that impossible. A twitter account is not enough. Soundbites cannot answer. It took me a lifetime and four books to understand and convey clearly enough that some might see past the absurdity.

The central problem that we face is not difficult to understand. Its resolution is startlingly simple. It is the delusions and broken thought processes that impede. We have been inundated with so much gibberish for so long that it makes it nearly impossible to peer through to the truth. Once one sees through to the primary delusion we have forced upon ourselves, the rest fall like dominoes.

I can, though, finally describe, in a succinct way, some of the after-effects of the primary delusion as I lead up to what is missing and the far more complex explanation of why.

Humanity has always attempted to *force* mankind to *act* as if it were human and sentient. We put laws in place to cudgel ourselves into *acting* human and sentient. That only puts a lid on the boiling cauldron of mankind. It does not improve anything. The cauldron blows its lid periodically as the delusions multiply and we continue to avoid our sentience.

We never even consider that mankind can just _be_ human, sentient, emotionally stable, reasonable, and sane. Not in some distant future but now. Our humanity has been maimed to the extent that we cannot even consider that the laws, rules, and regulations to restrain our inhumanity are for animals that do not inherently own their humanity.

Another after-effect of humanity remaining little more than a beast struck me long ago. We haven't progressed *as a species* for nearly three thousand years. My recurring question has always been *why*?

Any real progress towards a sentient state has been completely absent after our first foray into reason more than three thousand years ago. We've been at a virtual standstill regarding our sentient state ever since. We bandy about words that describe the finer qualities of being human but never attain them.

If one takes a close look at our recent situation and, then, compares it to our ancient history, one finds that we have not changed much at all. The material toys have become shinier and fancier, the deceptions more sophisticated, but humanity itself has hardly changed at all.

All of the less than satisfactory attempts at progress towards a sentient state, from psychiatry to psychology to sociology to banking to religion to the arts to governments to science, can be traced back thousands of years.

We tinker with these concepts as if they were the be-all and end-all of a sentient existence. We act as if hidden somewhere in their complexity is our sentience. As if the problem were not humanity itself but its constructs. Tinkering with these concepts makes us feel like we are doing something sentient and important, while all we are doing is continuing to attempt to mimic the sentient state while distracting ourselves from the real problem.

We abandoned our humanity before we ever got started. Instead, we have distracted ourselves by obsessing about the constructs and antics first created by a nearly witless animal that has refined itself into a demented animal. It has done little to get us any closer to being human.

The most important and revealing after-effect, is that we have created so many bizarre notions regarding love. This exemplifies our delusional state.

We have created the grave misdirection that love is nothing more than an intellectual exercise. The phrase "all we need is love" flips the situation on its head. It says that we need only think in a loving manner, imagine a loving state. *Aaarrrggghhhh!*

We don't need to *learn* to love, just as we don't need to learn to be human. In order to love, we need to *be* human by removing a single impediment to our humanity.

We create phrases like "love all" and "love conquers all". Our deluded state spawns the concept that love is no more than a thought process, a thing of will. That all we need to do is think in a loving manner, like a brute bashing his head against a stone until he breaks through. Then everything will be alright. The proof of error is in the millennia of failure.

Our sentient potential created the concept of love. We taste it, like a word on the tip of one's tongue. We know of its potential to exist and its importance to a sentient context but can never seem to attain it in full. Our delusions have made it a meaningless, ambivalent, ambiguous, confusing concept and prospect because we attempt to *force* the situation. The only difference between love and all of the other finer human qualities is that love sits at the center of a sentient existence. Love flourishes as a natural extension of sentience for the most astonishing reason that, in retrospect, is not astonishing at all.

Our bewilderment has caused us to downplay love and belie its significance. Many dismiss the idea of love as naïveté, a weakness, while unsuccessfully chasing it throughout a lifetime. We have put the concept of love through the grinder more than any other human quality. It has been degraded into a rotted version of the most tremendous, magnificent concept.

Love does not make us human. Attaining our humanity makes us capable and worthy of fulfilling love and able to recognize its true origin, meaning, potential, and worth.

The finer human qualities are not a set of clothes to be donned by an animal on a whim. Humanity will only be able to earn those clothes through the application of its sentient awareness and intellect to resolve one elusive issue: the origin of love.

We cannot imagine humanity unmarked by reprehensible behaviour. All the bread crumbs are there. We just need to follow them without the conditioning of fear and delusion.

Once we unleash ourselves from the straitjacket of the beast and no longer mimic a sentient state but fulfill it, our progress will be astonishing.

We can become human and that is more astonishing than anything one can imagine.

Back To The Drawing Board

After attempting to understand and explain, through three books and many decades, the ramifications of the dilemma that we have always faced, I'm finally beginning to understand just how difficult a task I set myself.

Surprisingly, the problem itself is not difficult to understand or resolve. Overcoming the delusions that reinforce the fearful desire to never face the problem is the monumental issue. The problem itself is very straightforward with a straightforward solution. The fabricated fictions we tell ourselves are the real problem. They make it nearly impossible to face the situation.

The delusions create a deep, baseless fear which makes us quake when considering the issue. We become mesmerized by the unsupportable conclusion that the problem is insurmountable. It is a challenge indeed to peer through and accept the essential truth: we have yet to unleash our sentience. It is easier to avoid the mirror than consider what is really wrong. This reflects all that is wrong with our condition.

The feelings of hopelessness regarding our predicament are passed on by each generation to the next. After a youthfully instinctive rebellion against the absurdity of it all, the fiction slowly insinuates itself into one's life in crushing defeat. It is not just hormones coursing through our body at puberty that create the rebellion. It is realization that something is missing.

In point of fact, everything can finally come together once we face a single baseless, destructive fear from our past. Confronting the gibbering beast's blinding, overwhelming fear changes everything.

We are *conditioned* to look away from the problem due to an underlying fear that it is insurmountable. ***It is not!*** This is why it has taken me four books to understand and explain it thoroughly. I had to face my own battles. I hope I am finally explaining in such a way that the desire to look away can be overcome. We can fulfill that which animals never even contemplate. Don't shy away because the subject matter makes you uncomfortable. Stand your ground.

Something has been holding us back from fulfilling our sentient nature. The attributes of heightened awareness and intelligence only create the *potential* for a sentient condition. They only give us the keys to unlock the puzzle. Once we unshield our awareness we can, then, utilize our intellect to overcome that which has been missing.

Here we go, again

Freud was right and he was wrong. He suggested that it was all about sex and that humanity's repression of sex is a problem. Those insights promises Freud a place in history for all time. The final result of the liberation that Freud began is humanity gaining a sentient perspective and becoming human, at last. He was wrong in that it is *only* all about sex until it isn't.

Freud could not comprehend that the repression of sex is a sign of something far more significant.

The next step was beyond him. It took many generations before we could ask *why* the human race represses sex? It is not just a few individuals, cultures, or belief systems. It is a worldwide phenomenon that spans all cultures and boundaries. It is such a vast phenomenon that it must be assigned to the whole race of humanity. Freud attempted to isolate it into quirks and perversions of individuals. His primary mistake was not addressing the repression of sex as a problem for the human race as a whole.

The Flower Power generation and the Summer of Love took it the next significant step and came achingly close. Unfortunately, they fell victim, naturally enough, to garbling what they sensed.

Even though they used the right words, they still missed by a mile. They said the words but did not follow through. This points to the depth of the delusions and subtle forces that encourage us to look away from sex. Free *Love*? Really?

They connected all of the right dots; love, sex, humanity, and the finer qualities of the human race; but still they couldn't quite put their finger on it. They felt the pulse but never reached the heart of the matter.

To get so close and still miss the mark is noteworthy. It's like it is on the tip of our tongue (no pun intended) and, yet, we can't quite find the words to express the reality, even when it is right there in front of us. Their proposal of 'Free Love' rebelled against the repression of sexuality, but went no further. Another crucial milestone, but not the last.

Even though the phrase they used was "Free *Love*", all they implemented was "free *sex*". They surrendered to the idea that *more* sex was the answer, only to be disappointed. Another generation conceded defeat to the beast in sheer consternation. It was a huge step forward but something remained missing. The beast won, again.

That generation created an important milestone in freeing humanity from its forced blindness regarding sex but, still, it gave no real answers and created further delusions. They deserve a place in history because they did not just open the door. They did not just knocked it down. They blew it apart. They came so achingly close to revealing what the hell is wrong with mankind. "Free Love" said it all and we still missed it. It was a generation that adamantly rebelled in full regalia against the fiasco of our failed sentient state. They came so very close (pun intended).

An interesting human potential is for eye to eye penetrative sexual intercourse. We are the only species that can consciously look into the eyes of our partner during sexual intercourse. *Yet, there is a desire to turn the lights out.*

The tendency to turn out the lights is reminiscent of the repression of sex. This presages the real problem that we have gone to ridiculous lengths to suppress.

A human is not fulfilled by rutting like an animal. Our tremendous sentient potential has always sensed this. Deep down inside, we all know this and it drives us crazy. As our sentient awareness becomes sharper (and our eyes open) we become even more aware that something remains missing. The staggering reality is that we sense something that goes well beyond sex but is entirely dependent upon it. We sense the lock and key to everything that sentience represents.

The tantalizing hint of something more is what drove Freud on. The vague sense that something can be liberated by sex is what the Flower Power generation anticipated. In every case, the conditioning to look away was just too much.

Repression is not the problem. Repression is only where the breach in our sentient ascendance began. The problem itself and, then, fear preceded repression.

The discord is caused by our unfinished sentient nature reaching for sentient fulfillment while desperately avoiding its source. For millennia, the witless beast has encouraged us to cringe away from a close inspection of sex. How utterly deluded we have been.

There are so many faces that one could put on this struggle. The rebellious youth, full of hormones, sensing that there is something more, while the aged slowly become thoroughly ensnared and convinced of the inevitability of all the misery we endure. Or, woman reaching for a peaceful coexistence and equality while man thrashes about.

Misogyny, domestic violence, and other quirks and perversions are just a few of the pervasive and disastrous results. They are only the most direct results. *Abundant* sex alone, so enthusiastically pursued by the Flower Power generation, does not answer.

In its current state, sex remains nothing more than an animal's rutting pursuit and we remain a rutting, demented (due to the fact that we know better) animal. More rutting does not alleviate the issue.

The absence of that which can make sex extraordinary for a sentient being must be acknowledged, accepted, and fulfilled. It alleviates our distorted condition.

Our sentient awareness (and, especially, eye to eye sex?) emphasizes that something is still missing and always has been, even for the animals that preceded us. Animals don't have the wit to care about what is lacking. That animal precedent is what made us stumble so severely so long ago.

Our ancient ancestors simply followed the animal's lead and continued to rut along, brushing off any thoughts that sex could be so much more. Their wit could not comprehend what their sentient awareness made evident.

We have the wit to realize that there is so much more to the act of sex. We also have the wherewithal to do something about it. This is what can differentiate us irrevocably from the common animal. Our sentience will not leave us alone until we face this challenge and do something about it.

"That's just the way it is!" is the hopeless, helpless animal screaming for relief from its sentient awareness rather than confronting its awareness of the situation and making something human from the act of sex.

We have thrashed about in our attempts to avoid acknowledging the simple missing element that makes sex human. This has forced us down some very strange and perverse roads. The real question remains. *Why?*

The answer becomes more obvious as our sentient awareness evolves and all of the absurdity comes into focus. The long struggle to overcome the forced obscurity finally reveals the answer with crystal clarity.

Sex remains mostly the dichotomy of an animal's rutting. Satisfaction and fulfillment are split between the two genders. The man invariably attains the physical satisfaction of climax while the woman attains the emotional fulfillment of providing climax for one's mate. That is rutting.

Mutual physical satisfaction and emotional fulfillment are the hallmarks of a sentient sexual endeavor. S*hared* satisfaction *and* fulfillment is making love. It makes us fully human and sentient. Do not brush this off. The desperate avoidance of this simple conclusion is the cause for the repression of sex and the source of our troubles. It staggers one to begin to realize just how important the conclusion is.

Let me be very specific about the definition of the term making love. Making love is *mutual* sexual satisfaction *and* emotional fulfillment that frees eye to eye sexual intercourse to become something fulfilling and sentient. It is not just rutting like an animal. Making love makes us human.

The vast vista of love in its entirety can only begin to instantiate once its physical manifestation is commonly fulfilled.

It is about loving, *not rutting*. Rutting does not create love. *Making* love does. Read that literally. *Make. Love.* Pause and consider the phrase *make love*, not the connotations but the literal meaning of the phrase.

Making love, mutual satisfaction and emotional fulfillment, is the catalyst that begins to release all of the varied forms of love that we have always attempted to describe, but never attained, beginning with self-respect.

If you find yourself turning away, that is just the conditioning kicking in. Stick with it. It's as real as concrete. In it lies the evolution of the species into something far more than an animal.

The startling realization is that the sexual expression of a sentient race is the catalyst for the full panoply of meaning contained in the term love and all of the finer human qualities beginning with self-respect. Amusingly, it's not even a new realization. The term 'make love' is a rather ancient term. Unfortunately, but not surprisingly, it was reduced to the most basic meaning of any form of sex.

Love's genesis is tied up in transforming the rutting of an animal into the human act of making love. Only because of the blinding fear of failure in our ability to transform the act of sex into something human did we fail to confront the truth and transform the act. We failed to transform sex and, thus, failed to become human.

The difference between rutting and making love is the difference that unleashes our sentience. Our sentience cannot begin to fulfill itself until this realization becomes part of the conscious awareness of the species. It is an evolutionary step.

That which caused difficulty in facing the challenge and achieving this transformation is rather obvious. Once inspected without prejudice or fear, it is also obvious that it is a mirage. The situation easily and quickly yields to success, once confronted without the baseless fear.

The ongoing failure to bring sex to a sentient conclusion is a crushing defeat and disaster for humanity. <u>The gibbering fear that instigated the defeat and impeded our progress towards a sentient state was that there was no reliable way for a man to attain physical satisfaction for the woman *during sexual intercourse*.</u>

The mind veers away from this conclusion. Men don't want to admit it and women have been trained not to mention it. Men lose their self-respect (and any chance of fulfilling higher ideals) and women become disillusioned and bewildered by men. There may be exceptions but they are few. If anyone has known the answer before now, they have not passed it on. Men decided they couldn't do any better and did not want it mentioned. We have danced around the subject for millennia.

That was a mistake of monumental and disastrous proportions. ***It is dead easy for any man to last as long as desired during penetrative sexual intercourse***. In so doing, we release our humanity, we become human.

Our nearly witless ancestors failed and, not only passed on the failure itself, but amplified the fear of failure to the point of paralysis, mania, and a fictitious sentient existence.

Give and take. With rutting, the woman gives and the man takes. That is an animal's purview. Making love means both give pleasure and both take emotional fulfillment.

It's no wonder we have been such a mess. We all feel gypped. Both genders fail to feel fulfilled. Our sentience has put us in the position of knowing there is so much more to sex than an animal ever dreamed of but we haven't quite reached out to make it real. Talk about a nightmare. We have thrashed around for more than three millennia attempting to avoid the truth because we just couldn't believe that sex could become something more and life could begin to fulfill. It is the step into our sentient state that completes us as sentient beings.

Once the fear is replaced by success, our sentient state will be fully awakened. All of the deceits, delusions, and absurdity of our current existence begin to fade away. The physical satisfaction of the woman spawns the emotional fulfillment of the man. This completes the cycle of sex and we become human. It is no longer all about sex.

We are human and sentient. We have the awareness to understand that something is missing from sex. We also have the intellect to do something about it. We can achieve the simple change required to make sex into something human or we can remain a befuddled monkey in its stupour.

The necessary transformation of our humanity is contained in the transformation of the act of rutting into the act of making love. That may sound simple and it actually is. It is only the cluster of nonsense, fear, and fictions that have bewildered us and prevented us from realizing just how important (and easy) it is to resolve sex into something human and sentient.

We have hesitated on the threshold of our sentience for more than three thousand years because our earliest ancestors feared they could never overcome the obstacle.

The potential for sentient fulfillment wasn't even a glimmer in their eye. Sex was just rutting. So be it. So, they just turned out the lights. Not important. Women's sexual fulfillment was relegated to the void.

Humanity becomes fully human when sex becomes more than a haphazard animal endeavor. It completes the humanity of both genders. The man becomes self-confident and emotionally stable by fulfilling their female partner's desire for sexual satisfaction. The woman is unleashed by finally achieving sexual satisfaction regularly in the intimate setting of a sexual encounter.

It is astonishing to realise that 'nature' (or whatever you wish to call it) created sex in such a way that a simple adjustment makes sex into something fulfilling in more ways than an animal could ever possibly imagine. Ironically, we have avoided fulfilling our sentience for all of this time by avoiding a close inspection of the sexual encounter.

We have always sensed this, which is clearly apparent in the ongoing struggle represented so well by Freud and the Flower Power generation. As we approached the truth, something has always driven us frantically away. An overwhelming fear precedes any deep consideration that sex could be something more. As one ponders, it becomes clear that sex is something important to our sentient ascendance.

The transformation of sex into something sentient begins an iterative process. Once sentient sex is fulfilled, it becomes all about love. It will no longer be just about sex. Sex will no longer be an obsession. Sex will be fulfilling and fulfilled.

Man can finally learn to love once he is successful at satisfying his female partner face to face. The woman's loving potential is unleashed and flourishes. Once sex becomes commonly fulfilling, we can begin to settle into being human and explore all of the facets of the word love that go so far beyond the scope of the couple to encompass our sentient potential.

It must be noted that sexual fulfillment is not the most important factor. It is the confident anticipation of sexual fulfillment that transforms the human race. In other words, we attain our sentient nature when sexual fulfillment becomes the commonly accepted and assured expectation. Every human becomes validated in its existence when fulfilling sex becomes expected and assured, even without consummation.

The repression, distortions, and many, many perversions regarding sex are only the most immediate of the horrible consequences of not achieving sentient sex. The dominoes fell far and wide. All of our surface issues are influenced by our past inability to achieve a sentient, loving perspective. They will also fall far and wide as we emerge into sentience.

Sentient beings are meant to create a loving environment, starting with the physical bonding between man and woman. Love is an advanced, more sophisticated form of caring that no simple animal could ever achieve. Love begins with the advanced, sentient form of sexual expression.

We begin to transcend the animal by realizing that there is so much more to sex than an animal can ever comprehend. The final result is complete comprehension of the tremendous prismatic aspects of love that we have hopelessly chased since we first gained our sentience.

The problem is that almost any man has (a completely _unnecessary_) difficulty in fully satisfying their mate during sexual intercourse. This is due to the (unnecessary) difficulty in remaining sexually aroused. The failure is just a remnant of the animal that a human can easily overcome.

While any form of sex that provides satisfaction for the woman is a tremendous step forward, only mutually satisfying penetrative sexual intercourse (especially eye to eye) completes the dual nature of satisfaction and fulfillment for both lovers. Looking into the eyes of the other during that fulfillment is the icing on the cake, the final fulfillment. Or, in juxtaposition, the inability to look one's lover in the eye while achieving one's own sexual satisfaction is a landmark failure that impedes the fulfillment of our sentience.

Because men have suppressed the issue, they have also avoided inspecting the issue. This alone has derailed its resolution. Men have been programmed to expect failure. They have felt helpless in the face of the compulsion to believe it is insurmountable. ***It is dead easy to resolve.*** It has always only been necessary to confront the failure without fear and prejudice in order to understand just how simple it is to overcome. It is all in the mechanics of the act of sex that become starkly obvious once embarrassment is put away.

Make no mistake, all men want to be good lovers. They only remain lousy lovers because they believe it is hopeless. They are so wrong.

Most men desperately attempt to *delay* ejaculation rather than avoid starting the process of ejaculation. That is another disaster of ancient origin. Attempting to delay ejaculation only delays the end a little. It is essential to never initiate the process of ejaculation!

There is a rather simple reason that the process of ejaculation begins. It has to do with a particular movement that has been trained into the male animal for millions of years. To put it most simply, *don't twerk until the lady sings!*

Because we are human rather than just an animal, we can adjust and avoid that particular motion until it is time to conclude the act of loving with full satisfaction and fulfillment. Please see the book, *Sentience*, for a more detailed explanation. There are many subtleties, such as the variance in the ease of a woman's arousal, that are worth knowing. as well, and is contained in the book.

While release of the ejaculate deep inside of the female is the primary goal for an animal, it is not the *only* sentient purpose for sex. For an animal, that *is* all there is to it: pump that ejaculate deep inside and make babies. For humanity, sex also begins the fulfillment of sentience.

The key that unlocks our sentience is as much the man's emotional fulfillment created by the sexual satisfaction of the woman as it is the physical pleasure of climax garnered by the woman. Both are essential to unlocking our full sentient state. The most disastrous result in its absence is the man's feelings of failure. Look around. The results are everywhere.

The failure is no more than a habit performed by men during sexual intercourse that has been repeated since long before humanity existed. The unsuspected habit that is almost an instinct induces the initiation of the process of ejaculation. Stop performing this single movement during sexual intercourse and a man stops the process of ejaculation in its tracks before it ever begins.

This inability to perceive the simplicity of the solution emphasizes the nature and depth of delusions and deceits we have indulged since the earliest days of our existence. The deceits cause such a disruption to our sentient condition that it destroys our sentient perspective.

Rutting like an animal is a matter of men *taking* satisfaction. The potential for love atrophies. Loving begins with *sharing* physical satisfaction, *making* love.

The more subtle observation regarding the nature of sex is another matter entirely. Making sex into something that a human can accept fulfills the human potential. It unleashes love. Denying the sentient awareness of the situation leaves us a demented animal.

The first generation to pursue this change will find it more challenging than later generations, because they will be overturning the imbecilic learnings, practices, and paradigms of thousands of years. It will take some time, patience, discipline, and practice for the first generation. As it becomes common knowledge, as it is passed down from father to son, as *sentient* manhood becomes confident in itself, it will become second nature to last as long as it takes to love.

The chapter in the book *Sentience* on Techniques and Considerations provides an in-depth description and understanding of what it takes for that first generation. The book explains in detail how a man can go about lasting as long as desired/required, as well as the simple mechanics of the situation. If you are intuitive enough, maybe you can understand without the book: *don't twerk until the lady sings.* It will be easier just to read the book.

Haven't you ever wondered why the education regarding sex that is available only describes the downsides, the dangers and how to avoid them?

Later generations will have no need for the book or instructions at all (though *real* sex education might be nice in the short term). In essence, it really is that simple. Confidence in the results will make it a simple, foregone conclusion for future generations that will take it for granted.

Fulfilled sentience is not something that will happen overnight but, the end result is certain. In the meantime, *couples* will become fulfilled. That's a good start.

Emotional stability and deep-seated self-confidence and self-respect are crucial results of learning to love. The ripple effects will journey far and wide throughout everything regarding the human race.

Like a troupe of Keystone Cops we have ironically and desperately avoided becoming human. Humanity has been driven insane by its own delusions that have forced us to avoid the central issue - men need to learn to perform sex differently from an animal. Men need to learn to make love. The act of making love initiates a loving environment.

I do not mean to blame men or anyone else. I can't even blame our ancient ancestors that started the ball of our demented state rolling. They were just as much a victim of circumstances. It's no one's fault but it's time to move on. The poem, *Desiderata,* comes to mind.

Women have carried the torch of our sentience and love since the beginning because, unlike men, they *never fail to provide satisfaction for their mate.* This is no great tribute to women. As with men, it is the inherited circumstances.

I suggest you pause here for a few days to let this all sink in. Maybe even go back and re-read these chapters. As you move forward from this point, I am much more blunt about what is going on. But, this is the essence. I have tried to be exceptionally careful and sensitive up until this point because of the delusions that need to be overcome. Please get well over the central delusions before proceeding past the poem.

Once mankind learns to make love, we become human and can proceed to fulfill the state of love which is far more than anything we ever imagined. Innocence is not naïveté, gullibility; love is not blind; life need not be an endless, hopeless, unmitigated misery and disaster. You can skip the poem, if you like.

"Whispered words"

Whispered were the words with which I spoke
Of grandness of humanity awoke
I faced the wounded wailing of the beast
And whispered of the way the nonsense ceased
Against the glowing galaxies so grand
In contrast to humanity unmanned
I whispered of a change within the state
A burning of the nonsense to ablate
Whispered words upon the winds that wait
Tell of humanity becoming great

Strange

It's strange but I feel like I still haven't made the results clear enough. It is just so clear in my mind, which makes it difficult to put into words.

Imagine a world where everyone comes to feel invalidated by the glorious expectations of sex that are never attained. As sex falls far short of everyone's expectation, we feel there is something wrong with us. We take it very personally. So, you have a world in which everyone is running around putting on a show that everything is alright, while they know it isn't. That is the Theater of the Absurd in which we live.

Now, imagine a world in which those expectations are fulfilled. A world in which there is no invalidation of the most fundamental act of being alive. Do I really need to say more than that? Do I need to detail how radically everything will change? Do I need to explain how those fumbling, awkward attempts, as we reach puberty, become replaced over time by wholehearted anticipation of something that we have finally learned will match our expectations? Can you begin to extrapolate the tremendous change from there?

Loneliness. We attempt to fill the void, left by sex that meets no sentient expectations, with the presence of others or many bizarre pursuits but it can only be fulfilled by completing our sentient selves. Many (maybe most) even feel lonely in the presence of others. The presence of others only adds to our fulfillment, once we feel validated, self-confident. *We must gain our self-respect first and the belief that it is all worth it.*

We attempt to fill that void in so many absurd ways. Nothing and no one can validate our existence for us. Plenty of situations and people can go a long way towards invalidating you in our current setup, if you let them. But, we can only validate ourselves.   Or, to put it in the usual vernacular. We have to love ourselves first.

It is so very strange that we *know* something is wrong. Believe me when I tell you, the immensity of the compulsion to avoid looking in the mirror nearly overwhelmed me.   It attacks below the threshold of awareness.   It tells you it's useless. There were alarm bells going off all over the place in my head, warning: do not consider this. Warning! Warning!

Luckily, I have trained myself for a lifetime to not accept bullshit when I hear it and, as I further uncovered what was really going on, my fury and outrage sustained me. The process of discovery made it easier to persevere as the immensity of the absurdity became increasingly apparent.

I still worry greatly, though, that I will not be able to prevent those warning bells from going off for anyone else. I have done everything I can in the previous pages to mute those misleading alarms. If you've gotten this far, it is very likely I have been successful.

The three previous books are another matter. They are best read *after* this book. My fury and outrage is much more prevalent in the previous books. It was necessary. The four books comprise my own learning process. If one is interested in delving further into the bizarre situation and my own process of overcoming the obscurity created by millennia of absurdity, the other books may be of value. Somebody reading any of the previous books first will have to have some serious stamina and an incredibly open mind to persevere.

The book *Sentience* is another matter entirely. It has its own reasons for perusal. Still, for now, it is best to read this book first.

Believe me, I went through the same necessary process of expulsion of the absurdities. It's not an easy task.

We shake our heads in acceptance of the debacle of our current existence. I still shake my head. The difference is that I don't accept the absurdities as fait accompli. Everyone seems content to rant about our lunacy while they drown in its midst. So, excuse my occasional explosions of fury while writing about the results of the stupour we embrace. It just becomes too much for me on occasion.

No one seems to wish to look at what is really going on or even entertain that there is a real answer to our dilemma. Everyone seems totally convinced that we are little more than a demented animal and there is nothing to be done about it. I could litter pages with the many, many reactions to our bizarre state of existence that answer nothing.   Everyone seems to cling to their very own version in desperation.

Blowing apart the door of our delusions, as the Flower Power generation did, is worth a little closer examination at this point.

Behind all of the prim and proper absurdity of the past is a seething mess that is seldom acknowledged.   It exemplifies our mimicry of a human, sentient being.

The prim and proper attitude attempted to avoid accepting just how rampant perversions, misogyny, sexism, and domestic abuse are.   It attempts to convey that it is all somebody else's problem.   Right.

It is not inaccurate to say that perversions, misogyny, sexism and domestic abuse rule our very existence to a great extent.   We fight on desperately against something which never should have existed in the first place.   It is fighting against a demented animal.   One doesn't win such a fight. The derangement must be eliminated.   The human must take its place.   We have never peered below the surface of these acts of insanity to understand what is really wrong.

Why do perversions, misogyny, inequality, and domestic violence even exist?   Why are they persistent traits of mankind?   They are the persistent traits of a demented animal.   Why would they ever possibly develop in the first place?   They are not natural and, yet, they are pervasive.

They obliterate a sentient context for our existence but they are not the source of the obliteration.   They are just symptoms.

It is the perfect camouflage.   Between the comfortable familiarity of our delusions and the fear instilled in us, we are left with vague answers filled with deception and bewilderment. We remain a bewildered beast.

We suggest it is the problem of certain individuals.   Prim and proper folks don't have these problems. *Right*. The prim and proper attitude, the righteous, sanctimonious attitude is just another symptom, hiding much more than it reveals. These problems exist *because* we blinded ourselves to the truth. It is *humanity*'s problem and we fight against it rather than realizing it has no good reason to exist in the first place. You see? There's that fury and outrage, once again.

Questioning our existence

Men have a simple problem which betrays mankind's sentient nature, destroying it in the process. It is a process of disaster. The problem makes men feel deceitful. Because they feel deceitful, it leads to the erosion of their honesty and integrity. This leads to the delusions and their helpless acceptance of the problem, which leads to further delusions, which further erodes our state, etc, etc, etc. The initial failure makes men feel unworthy of a woman's love which leads to the upheaval of the relationship between sexes and the rest of the dominoes continue to fall. Men do not know love.

The key question that I have always been attempting to answer is what is wrong with humanity? Surprisingly, even to myself, I found the answer! Rephrasing the question slightly makes it easier. What is wrong with *man*kind?

The false front that men erected (there's a pun in there somewhere), from time immemorial, was first created as they became aware of their lack and tried to hide it rather than overcome it. Earliest man, with wit comparable to a great ape or a rock, just could not cope. From there, it was all downhill.

There is no doubt that we made a grave mistake and, yet, we have danced around the truth for millennia. It is everywhere to see and, yet, we hem and haw about it. We politely avoid the issue entirely. Yes, women can be vituperative, as well, but that is a result of the state that men's situation has created. In any instance, the difference between the detrimental impact of men on our situation and that of women is like comparing a supernova to a firefly.

Men do not need pills, surgery, appliances, or complicated positions in order to overcome an animal's limitation regarding sex. We are *not* just an animal. That we haven't even seriously considered the difficulty, much less resolution, emphasizes the fact that we have remained in denial.

Make no mistake, men are lousy at sex, just like most male animals. The differences that distinguish humans are that 1) our awareness of the lack cannot be avoided because of humanity's heightened awareness. That is a blessing, not a curse. It is what makes us human. And, 2) humanity's enhanced intelligence means that men can do something about it. That is what confirms man's humanity. What is also surprising is that evidence regarding what it takes to be good at sex is all around. Because of the fear instilled many millennia ago, we have avoided what is right before our eyes.

The conundrum is that men have not done anything about it because our ancestors were willing to bury the problem due to shame long ago. That ridiculous shame remains unchecked, even today.

Men being bad at sex is not something to be ashamed of, though that has been the relentlessly ongoing reaction due to the defenses that have continued to build up the conditioning that avoids the issue entirely.

Sometimes I wonder if the only reason (besides the conditioning) that men have not ever become good at sex is that no one considers it a serious problem. Do we just brush it off, never considering its importance to our diminished state of sentience? In media, it is often treated like a joke. Women aren't laughing. They are finally finding alternatives.

Women have not made a big deal out of it in the past, excusing it and giving the male gender the benefit of the doubt (or also considering it hopeless, just like men have). It has taken the female gender more than three thousand years to finally begin to get fed up enough with all of the excuses that accrue regarding the male gender. It's about time.

Those excuses that women have tolerated and helped create are one of the original misdirections that have only become increasingly leveraged over time. There is probably good reason for women avoiding confronting the issue in the past. They were probably beaten near death if they ever mentioned it.

Make no mistake. It's no joke. The inability to fulfill the physical promise of love creates the upheaval that we have endured since the beginning and abruptly ends any chance at understanding the full nature of love or sentience.

Sex is not a curse on mankind. Rutting is. Sex, as it was handed down to us from the animals that preceded us, is just incomplete. It is not evil. It is just in a simplified form that mankind can improve on.

Sharing sexual satisfaction and emotional fulfillment definitively distinguishes the human from any other animal. Loving sex creates the loving state. It fulfills the promise of love and fills in, as well as unleashes, our sentient state.

Let's be blunt

The evidence for our condition, in which we never achieved our humanity, is downright blatantly, sickeningly, surprisingly, obvious. Domestic violence and its slightly slightly lesser derivative, misogyny point directly at the problem. The excuse-laden persona of the male gender is laid bare.

These sickening portrayals of the human species are the first symptoms of the problem. That we accept these abhorrent reactions of violence and hate without any deeper thought than that they are abhorrent only makes sense within the backdrop of failed sentient sexual intercourse. We never question the existence of these horrible traits of mankind. We just accept them as fait accompli or soft-sell them. *Why?*

Ask yourself. What else, other than men's awareness of their failure to attain sentient sex, could possibly be responsible for the horrible acts of domestic violence and misogyny? *Don't* underestimate their pervasiveness (or men's overwhelming predominance in domestic violence) in all its forms from physical, mental, and verbal violence to the violence of brute domination and pompous, jeering, offensive behaviour. It all has the same source that *need not exist.*

Misogyny and domestic violence are not isolated incidents involving a handful of executives, rock stars, or politicians. These are just the most blatant, over-the-top examples that hit the press. They are just examples of men that have become fully engaged in the heinousness, due to positions of leverage, where they need not restrain their vicious behaviour. Read the Simone de Beauvoir quote. It is a much more accurate quote regarding power than the usual one.

Many cultures have even settled into a seemingly formal truce between the two genders. That still is not a solution.

These are pervasive, male gender-spanning behaviours that affect the whole race of humanity. This is most blatant in more primitive cultures. We haven't grown out of them. We have only learned to disguise them. That is not an answer. Men just become increasingly embarrassed by their behaviour as a culture becomes more sentient, so the failure goes underground. That's not a good thing.

The club has been turned in for other tools. Some men just get more carried away with the false front of their portrayal of the disgusting animal and equate it with masculinity. They let their money, power, fame, or intractability talk. Mostly, misogyny and domestic violence are just so offensive that they become indulged in private, behind the curtain. Many of the attributes of sexism, though, cannot be hidden so easily. All of it eventually goes underground. That does not resolve the issue.

Some men, mostly due to circumstances, seem to do a great deal better at dealing with the corrosive force. That does not mean the corrosive force is not present. For some, their intellectual understanding of how humans should behave overrides the worst of the behaviour.

Sorry to say, but a man being trained into his humanity by a woman is just mimicking the reality. Women thinking they can train men to be human is one basis for our bizarre experiment of *acting* human.

That intellectual understanding of how to be human must be transformed into an inherent feeling of validation and self-confidence. It *needs* to become the natural state of being human. There is only one way that happens.

The confident persona that all men attempt to portray must become the confident essence of human consciousness, not the carefully contrived strut and swagger of a brute. That brutish, outwardly displayed false confidence must disappear from the world stage. In so doing, the Theater of the Absurd will be closed permanently.

The worst representatives of the gender become ruthless, lying machines bent on destruction, as the appalling truth remains deeply embedded in their subconscious. The alpha male tradition of animals proving their manhood has transformed, in humans, into sickening, alternative ways to avoid the issue at hand and just further derail our humanity. The demented animal remains.

Egalitarianism

Can you think of any rational reason why the male gender of a race of consciously thinking beings would desire to dominate their female counterparts? Wouldn't it make a great deal more sense for men to please women? For the two sexes to work alongside each for the benefit of the race? What prevents this from occurring? Why the prevalence of misogyny and domestic violence instead? The idea that women should ever have had to fight for their rights is utterly insane. Those rights should have never been in question.

There is only one answer that suits. The sentient awareness of men *knows* they are not pleasing the woman and react badly to the situation. There are so many examples with regards to the character of men. All of the crude jokes and braggadocio of men comes to mind. But, I won't get into that in this book. It's covered well elsewhere while I was even more prone to rant.

Don't give me that old saw about improvement of the human race. That men need to be assholes in order to get the 'best' women and improve the race. Do we really look like we are improving? Or, do we look like a bunch of animals looking for excuses for our horrible behaviour? We can continue to bury ourselves behind facades and go on as something less than human or we can change.

Why in the world should women ever have had to fight for their rights? The proposition underlines the insanity.

Egalitarianism is the obvious choice for a sentient race. Respectful cooperation is sentient. The division between the genders is becoming more and more like armed camps of the wholly demented animal. That we don't inhabit an egalitarian existence points directly to the problem at hand.

Men have a problem that they have not faced, do not want it mentioned in any way and, thus, we all react badly. It seems easier to sweep the whole problem under the rug. Ironically, it is the problem that all men dearly desire to overcome and, yet, in our stupour, we remain frustrated and aggravated instead. We remain less than human.

Read *Sentience* if you as a man or your man cannot last as long as desired during sexual intercourse. It will take time, effort, patience, discipline, and practice for the first generation, but it is dead easy to overcome. It is crucial that it become common knowledge in order for mankind to finally become human and distinguish itself from animals.

Loving sex is a difference that, once humanity embarks on the course, completely differentiates us from the animal. We have the potential to be far more than an animal. All we need to do is take this easy step forward.

Once the race of humanity attains its sentience, there will be no backsliding. It is a step into our sentient state that will not be undone by any cataclysm (and avoids the self-induced versions).

Do not feel that you are alone if you are a man and suffer from the inability to last as long as it takes to thoroughly sexually satisfy a woman and *don't* make the mistake of thinking that, if you struggle to last a little longer, that is good enough. You should be able to last as long as you desire without *any* difficulty.

The key

In retrospect, it will be no surprise at all that it is sex that unlocks our sentience. Sexual repression and the bizarre attributes assigned to sex are a dead giveaway. Our whole horrific history of sex is a dead giveaway.

In the meantime, it will be such a shock that few humans will initially believe it - because they hide from any close inspection of the sexual situation. Too many are convinced that sex is evil, the original sin and all that. Too many others avoid thinking about it at all. Many, many have accepted alternatives in their desperate desire for physical contact and love and will have difficulty accepting that love between man and woman can ever succeed. Many think the problem is personal, as if they are the sad exception.

We have so immersed ourselves in the state of a bewildered animal, nodding our heads like a bobble doll, that it will be nearly impossible for many to see through the delusions to what is obvious: humanity can be a rational, emotionally balanced, loving, confident, sentient race. Now. Not in some vague, distant future.

We can keep fooling around thinking its normal for a sentient being to murder, kill, lie, cheat, steal, and, otherwise, act heinously, or we can finally become human. Those heinous acts are the actions of a race of beings that is essentially frothing at the mouth. Don't blame it on a few individuals, don't point to individual heinous acts as if they were the exception. Don't think that laws and regulations really change anything at all. Look at the panorama for the first time in your lives. Some of the most heinous and detrimental acts are enacted by the wealthy. Find an alternative explanation for that.

Do you really think that a race in full possession of its sentient faculties; with a stable emotional state, an egalitarian perspective, and its sanity in tact; would tolerate the current human conditions of crime, poverty, starvation, mindless leaders, and environmental damage? It is the conditions and conduct of an out of control race heading into a train wreck.

Do not try to feed me the line that it will all trickle down and everything will be alright or that holding everyone's hand will make it all okay. Those are both childish ramblings of a demented beast mimicking a human. They are meant to soothe the masses while pocketing the spare change.

In the modern world very few of the heinous acts have anything to do with survival. While that is often the justification, it has everything to do with a human race that is off the rails. They are the actions of a beast that has been driven insane by avoiding its sentience.

As I finally really understood what was going on, I had to think long and hard on the following question. Do I despise the human race? The answer is a resounding no. But, I utterly, deeply, with every fiber of my being, deplore the human condition. It is a sad excuse for a sentient race.

Keeping up appearances

It is almost certain that some man, with his carefully contrived swagger and mocking substitute for true manhood, that false front that desperately attempts to mimic the real thing, will pompously and loudly proclaim, "But, men are meant to rule, not love" or some other such nonsense.

But, you see, that's the point. They are thoroughly embarrassed by their unnecessary inability to love. Many are so far gone that they can't even contemplate love seriously.

The predicament will not go away on its own. Men have been hiding from it since day one. The failure makes all of *man*kind, masculinity, and humanity into a lie. The absurdity is that all they ever needed to do was face the issue.

Whether it is the man with his carefully contrived swagger, or the bookworm that hides from life, or the man begging for forgiveness, they are all embarrassed by their inability to make love. *Everyone* is only keeping up appearances.

Sentience's detractor

I am struck by the fact that things are already changing rapidly. I have read so many articles lately that finally underline the fact that few women ever achieve orgasm during sexual intercourse.

It is women that are finally stating the obvious. What is shocking (and personally frustrating), though, is that the central tenet for why that is true remains unstated. Women explain it every which way but never get to the point. Men are lousy at sex! Are they just being polite?, one of the traits of their inherent humanity. Is it the fear of repercussions or that nothing can be done about it that causes them to avoid stating the obvious? Success for men must become the common expectation in order for us to finally fulfill our sentient state. Otherwise, the sexes remain in armed camps.

I can certainly understand fear of the fallout of the mass reaction of men to any such statement, as well as a sceptical view regarding the claim that any man can be good at sex.

What is becoming glaringly clear, though, is that women are tired of it. It is unavoidable that we face the underlying truth of our situation, sooner or later. It is crucial that we also face the further truth that is there is no reason for *any sentient being* not to engage in loving sex!

It's just that everyone needs to look a lot closer at what is really going on in order to understand. Instead, because of our conditioning (and thousands of years of repetition), we are convinced that men cannot do any better. We have thrown up our hands in surrender, and wail and scratch our eyes out rather than face the issue.

In the absence of fulfilling sexual intercourse, the animal in us wins the field and will continue to do so until we fulfill our sentience by turning sex into a loving endeavor.

That fear of failure engenders all of the horrible antics of mankind that we see every day. The confusion, the paranoia, the violence, the willingness to accept failure at being human, the deception. As the failure seeps into a human's consciousness over a lifetime, they turn away and becomes something less, something distorted, something animal-like.

Hunger

We all have a hunger for love in its broadest sense, as well as its narrowest sense. It is built into our sentient state. We sense the potential but we have never really been able to attain it. We mimic what we know the human state should be and fail miserably. As we age, we give up the goal, finally accepting it as a nonsensical dream. We finally accept the disaster as inevitable. We surrender to less than the loving dream.

Love is inherent in the sentient model of existence. In their heart of hearts, women know it because, in the heightened state of sentient awareness, their ability to sexually satisfy their lover makes it overwhelmingly apparent. Their bafflement at our failed state of sentience is more than understandable.

It won't be nearly as difficult to perceive (or overcome) for those who do not grow up amidst the clutter of absurdity that we have thrown up in order to obfuscate the situation. It is only the slowly developed obscurity that we erected that has blinded us and made resolution seem impossible. In fact, the situation will be so very obvious that our descendants will be appalled at the muck their sad ancestors had to live through and baffled that it took so long for humanity to become human.

The obscuring delusions and deceptions have invaded every aspect of humanity's progress, turning our existence into a sad caricature of a sentient state. The paradigms and conditioning that mislead us manifest themselves in every way. We are so deeply embedded in an animalistic viewpoint, that it seems natural. The confusion has permeated every aspect of our existence making it difficult to isolate the fundamental cause, which was masked by the original, absurd intent of hiding it.

What happens when we finally lose all of our angst, paranoia, intolerance, and other animalistic bewilderments? What happens when we finally love rather than indulge the primary source of our agitation repetitively throughout a lifetime? What happens when misogyny and all of the varying aspects of sexism, that lie so close to the root cause, suddenly ceased to exist, because we removed their root cause?

Everyone can look around and identify many, many supposed sources of agitation. Look closer and the real nature and source of the agitation is revealed. If a person were emotionally stable and reasonable would those fabricated sources of agitation agitate? What really disorients our sentience so thoroughly? What really causes our sentience to go awry?

Look real closely at any of the divisions that separate us into smaller categories than just a single human race of sentient beings and you will, once again, see nothing but nonsense. Do any of them make the slightest bit of sense? The justifications for each are the preposterous proclamations of an animal.

Would the barriers erected between us and frustrations that we grasp at in desperation make sense for a rational, stable human? We love to blame our emotional state for our problems. Emotions are not the problem. It is the *instability* of emotions that causes our problems.

Look really deeply and you will begin to realise that we are all human and the human race, so far, is a failure. "We are all human" seems like an unnecessary phrase and it would be if it weren't for the agitation that destabilizes our emotional state on a daily basis, creates a paranoid perspective of distrust that regularly runs rampant, and renders any chance at a rational, emotionally stable state of existence impossible in its presence. It is a much better phrase than the absurd, "We are *only* human."

an animal trait that haunts us

We mimic being human while retaining a trait that is pure animal. It must be superseded by a sentiently aware race that recognizes the lack and overcomes it. So far, our sentient awareness has helplessly watched from the suppressed sidelines of our minds as the trait continues to derail us. It desperately needs to be addressed.

There is so much misery that clings to humanity. If one doesn't look closely, if one is blinded by the blur we superimpose on our sentient state, it seems inevitable. Take a closer look. It is all a facade behind which resides joy.

Cumulative Errors

Over the millennia, the errors have accumulated from the initial error of avoiding learning how to make love. This has created a fictionalized version of the sentient state that has nothing to do with our potential, but has to do with its abdication. It has everything to do with destabilized heightened awareness and intellect. It has to do with using our heightened conditions of awareness and intellect, in most cases, just to create destruction and further our delusions.

The phenomenon has only become emphasized by the web and our growing inter-connectedness. We are learning how to completely fictionalize our existence. In essence, *everything* is fake news, starting with the assumption that the human condition of misery and slapstick incompetency is inherent.

And their removal

A man physically satisfying his mate is just the start. As men gain their self-confidence through sexually pleasuring their mate, further impact is assured, as they become human. Their emotions are no longer in hiding. Just attempt to conceive of the further ramifications of men gaining a true sense of self-confidence and self-respect. They are vast.

A concise history of humanity

Three thousand years and we still haven't gotten it right. We still have not freed our reason, sanity, and love; our sentience. If you think, as you look around at the antics of mankind that we are sane, loving, or think with reason, you live in a different world than me, a fictional world.

Our history as a fully sentient race has not even begun. The deluded, dimwitted monster that mankind has portrayed for the last few thousand years has been the ongoing history of the unrelieved stupour engendered by our inability to face the gaping hole in our sentient awareness. It is time to overcome the dimwitted approach of an animal.

We just never realised that the dumb beast in us had long ago, through deception, distraction, and delusion, convinced us to remain an animal, thus forcing us to wear our mantle of sentience askew. The sentient being trapped within has never even suspected the amazing possibility of a rational, emotionally stable, loving existence.

It is time for the history of humanity to begin.

The answer

Altogether, over the long years, we have been waking up to the fact, in so many ways, that humanity, sentience, and reality are not what they seem. Underlying that simple statement is the unparalleled deception in our existence that is not easily overcome. Let me be crystal clear. The *deception* is not easily overcome. The *dilemma itself* could not be much easier to overcome.

The ripples of distortion that have torn through everything we conceive about humanity, sentience, and reality have compromised our ability to perceive the ease with which our existence as a sentient being can be fulfilled and the disturbing consequences of not fulfilling it.

We have fought tooth and nail to attain our sentient state without success because we have always misperceived it as a fight, a struggle to become sentient. While in fact, it has always been just a matter of unflinchingly facing the central issue, the root cause of our demented state. We needed to quit lying to ourselves. Sex needs to become more than rutting, more than just the satisfaction of the male. It is essential that heterosexual intercourse becomes loving.

The central issue is not something about which to be upset. It is not something of which to be embarrassed. *It is something for a sentient race to overcome and is easily done!*

The circle of confusion

It is like this crazy self-sustaining illusion regarding sex that becomes more confused the longer we look.

As an example, someone is writing a steamy romance novel or script concerning un-throttled passion and fulfilling sex. They know what good sex is *supposed* to be like. They've heard about it often enough. The guy lasting all night. The fervor beyond belief. The woman enjoying every moment. If they wish to sell the story and it involves sex, they have no option but to write it that way. It has to be written with fantastic sex - *whether the person writing it has ever experienced it or not.* The same is true of the actors. Many must groan in chagrin at acting out the part.

It's not even dishonest in that they are not saying they've ever received or given fantastic sex. They are just convinced that there is something wrong with them and do not realise it is something that is wrong with a great many (and, very probably, the vast majority of) relationships and our very state of existence. It's just a fictional account, right? It surely has happened to someone sometime, right? So, on it goes.

The circle of confusion progresses from there with no way out until we look seriously in the mirror.

Do me one favour. If you have never, or virtually never, received (or given) fantastic sexual intercourse (depending on your gender), believe your own experience over the fictions you see on tv and in movies. It really is the common experience. Don't think you are an oddity.

If you always give and receive superb sexual intercourse, that's a different story. I would dearly love to hear about it. I am only talking about the loving tangle of penetrative sexual intercourse because that is what is missing. Any alternative manner of both achieving orgasm is all well and good but only a limited version of the full expression of physical love. It is better than no physical pleasure for the woman, but provides limited emotional fulfillment for the man.

The fact is that I have already talked to a number of people about it. While everyone is absolutely convinced that bad sex can't be that common, not a single one of them had *ever* had sexual intercourse that fulfilled both.

What's wrong with us? Why are we so willing to believe fictional stories instead of our own experience? We have been bashing our heads against the wall for no good reason. We should have figured out a long time ago that intercourse is very often a bust and just how easy it is to make it a good experience. Everyone should be having it!

Big picture

As I continue to shed the absurdity and get beyond it to the idea that we can actually become a sane race, I realise that it is really about sentient evolution, which has nothing to do with further changes to our genes or our material welfare. It is about a different form of evolution.

It is about fulfilling the sentient awareness that revealed the concept of love and hints at the finer human qualities. Those finer qualities are so important that we haven't even begun to understand their full ramifications. It is about evolution of the conscious mind beyond that of an animal. We have been bounded by the self-inflicted deceptions that have caused us to become and remain a demented animal. It's a big step to become a fully sentient race.

What I have suggested and written only comprises the first step in a wholly transformative journey that is led by all of humanity. Humanity can finally guide itself beyond what closely resembles a gibbering beast.

Celebration versus despair

Have you ever noticed how mankind goes through these cycles of (seeming) celebration and (genuine, but unnecessary) despair? The former usually happens after a rather cataclysmic man-made event like WWII. We celebrate that, once again, we survived mankind's insanity just as if we had really rid ourselves of that insanity. And, then, sure enough, as predictable as the sunrise, the poison seeps back into mankind to lead it to despair, once again, as it realises it has not really improved one iota.

I gained the most fascinating insight from an experience in South Korea. The people of South Korea fascinate me. They just seem to pursue life and happiness with abandon. One day, I was sitting somewhere in Seoul and happened to be looking at a map of the area. It suddenly struck me. About 30 miles away was North Korea with missiles and millions of military personnel just waiting to pounce. It hit me that the reason they were so celebratory was the potentially pending doom that hung over them, much like the usual celebration and pending doom of mankind taking place simultaneously.

Humanity needs to achieve a true celebratory sense that it has overcome its demented traits without the impending doom hanging over our heads, without the doomsday clock only a few seconds away from midnight, or the escape of a fantasy fictional world, or the paranoias and delusions that create the desire to retreat into some fictional past where everything was better, where miracles were performed daily or life was a wonder. We are so close to exiting the fiction.

conditioning and paradigms

Paradigms are like a short-hand that replaces thinking in order for each of us to carry on with life. We make assumptions, react to life based on those assumptions, and seldom question them. They allow us to operate without stopping to think about each and every step in life that we take, both literally and metaphorically. They become a knee-jerk reaction. We will always have paradigms. It is just that those early paradigms in childhood become accepted premises before they can be regulated by critical thinking. Broken role models become accepted just as, upon the appearance of puberty, the broken model of sex becomes accepted. Our earliest ancestors found it easier to explain away lousy sex than to admit that something was missing. It must be a curse. We were born into sin. God meant us to be all fucked up. How could they possibly know that transforming sex could make all the difference in the world?

Those early paradigms continue to mislead us terribly. They act to allow the beast to remain. They undermine our critical thinking and predominate our lives.

We are all influenced by the paradigms created by our ancient ancestors. They acts as a comfort zone of delusions to enhance and embellish our fictional version of sentient reality, while the real world crumbles around us. The absurdity created by these paradigms and conditioning becomes more evident as our lives proceed.

Replacing these with healthy, sound, sane sentient paradigms will help make our condition whole and overrule the absurdity cluttering our lives.

The arguments between conservatives and liberals are an example of the results of these paradigms. The predominant assumptions of the arguments emphasize the misconceptions of our sentient state. The arguments never end because they are meaningless, they are the noises of the mimicking beast.

I never bought into any of it. While I was being told, "take a side", I was looking deeper.

high farce

I've mentioned in the previous books quite often that the human condition is utterly absurd. Not humanity's nature, just the current conditions in which we imitate the Keystone Cops.

As one studies current through ancient history more thoroughly, it's even worse. It is more like high farce. The antics of the animal get worse as the potential for damage becomes more significant. The erosion of our sentience continues as we drown in our stupour with no way out.

The only rather new, very scary proposition is the growing justification of the egoistical approach as the only rational approach. It is the highly irrational approach of a deranged animal. "Only the strong survive", rule, succeed. That is true as long as the human race remains as insightful as a bag of rocks and more vicious than any animal. There is no room for the finer qualities of humanity as we remain an animal.

Day by day, we further convince ourselves that we are no more than a beast. We are not just an animal. We can become so much more. The dimwitted state of humanity, that has so frustrated my own life, is not a terminal condition.

Good guys and bad guys

What really cracks me up about this crazy condition that we excuse as being human is that everybody is a good guy and a bad buy. It just depends on which side of which fence you view the situation. Everyone considers themselves the good guy as well as those with similar thoughts and interests.

It is true anywhere on Earth, in any country, religion, or other stupour-based and defined schism you choose. In this paranoid depiction of humanity, anyone who disagrees is bad.

Those folks that are fleeing some conflagration (usually to some 'advanced' society that has supplied arms to their home that is mired in conflagration). They're the bad guys.

The people from some other religion are, by definition, bad guys or - using the seemingly kinder view that people use only when forced to - just misinformed. When feeling really holy, they are tolerated. Their god is a delusion. Only one's own god is the correct view. Everybody else has it wrong. Sure. Some god that is.

The country that uses some other form of government that, by definition, isn't as good as yours. They're the bad guy.

Of course, you are the bad guy to each of those opposing schisms. Everyone is so confident that their way is the right! Makes me want to simultaneously cry or laugh.

The ones that really irritate me, with their embarrassing gross ineptness at being human in any way, are the ones that attempt to capitalize for their own personal gain. Whatever they are selling, *they're the bad guys*. I despise them with every fiber of my being. They are self-involved psychotic sociopathic, pathological liars and narcissists. Errr, egoists.

I guess you can't even imagine a world in which there are no bad guys, no evil. No one ever writes a *fictional* account of such. It takes more than simpleton imagination to conceive of a world with no bad guys.

Let's be clear. There never were bad guys. There are just a bunch of non-sentient beings running around attempting to act like they are sentient and doing a horrible job at it. It takes more than imagination to get past that obstruction.

resolution

I have been telling myself for awhile now that it's okay if I don't get through to humanity. We are headed in the right direction and will get there sooner or later. Even if I drop dead of a heart attack. Buddha, Freud, the Flower Power movement, all had the right idea, only missing the key that unlocks the love that fulfills our sentience. Love *and* sex. Not as two separate entities but combined in a loving tangle.

The breakthrough will happen. At least, I hope that is true, though I am no longer so sure. Look at what has happened over the last hundred years or so.

Maybe the most significant event over the last hundred years is the openness that has occurred regarding sex. Yet, we are still in denial regarding the actual problem. The blindness is heartbreaking. We come so close and veer away.

Sometimes, it seems we are just adamant about *not* facing the truth. We concoct pills that only further deform masculinity. We desperately look for any alternative rather than fix heterosexual penetrative sexual intercourse. One step forward, two steps back. How can we be so terribly blind??!?! *Aaaarrrggghhh!!!! Again!*

The inadvertent propagation of the myth of the inevitability of our poor performance (at sex and as a sentient race) are so well entrenched that it seems it will require a glaring light put on it in order to get to the crucial truth. That is what I am attempting to do. I've thought about writing it in blood on the front of my house and leaving my body as testament but, no, I've given a lifetime as it is, I won't give my death, as well. If it didn't seem so tacky, so crass, I might.

I am also beginning to realise just how ensnared we are. The fiction of our potential for only low achievement, with nothing greater in sight, is littered throughout our history. To see through those fictions that are induced by past fictions (!) is a challenge indeed. Every time you begin to see past the nonsense, you will be confronted with more fictional accounts that will make you question the reality that we must eventually admit in order to become human.

Dukkha

There is a word in the Buddhist belief system that is quite intriguing in the context of what I have been attempting to explain. Like Pandora's Box and The Garden of Eden, which I explained in *A sentient perspective*, it basically tells us what is wrong if we are only willing to open our eyes. It is utterly fascinating to me how the earliest myths came so close to the truth. After that, the impetus to veer away and never look in the mirror became stronger. We substituted pure nonsense for the truths that the myths were attempting to reveal.

The fascinating Buddhist belief is Dukkha. Samsara is the Buddhist belief in the endless cycle of birth, death, and rebirth (i.e reincarnation) which leads to the intriguing concept of Dukkha that just amuses me no end. Dukkha is defined as the innate characteristics of this existence. Dukkha defines the characteristics of life as suffering and *the incapacity to satisfy!!* They nailed it and we looked away!

Worldwide, it's pretty standard to believe that life equals suffering. Even atheists seem to like the idea of "Life sucks and, then, you die." or "Life is pain" if you'd rather. But, Dukkha notes the concept of the incapacity to satisfy! Considering the convoluted efforts of Kama Sutra that were created at about the same time in history in the same region of the world in an attempt to provide sexual satisfaction, it is straightforward that Dukkha is referencing the woman's missing sexual satisfaction. The people of that part of the world did better than anywhere else on Earth at attempting to address the problem of lousy sex with Kama Sutra.

Unfortunately, it does not really resolve the problem. Only "don't twerk until the lady sings" will do that. But, it's probably great aerobics exercise.

Can you break though to admit to yourself what "incapacity to satisfy" causes the disappointment, disruption, and upheaval of our humanity? Can you admit that it has no rational reason to exist? Think as hard as you might, can you think of one good reason why men cannot learn to last?

Don't even mention that it's all we've ever known. We have never even acknowledged it as a defining difference between humans and animal. We have never really tried. How could we possibly overcome it when we are not even willing to admit it? We just rut, become frustrated, and accept it as fait accompli.

Most important to emphasize is that our awareness of the situation is complemented by the other characteristic that separates us from animals: our intellect. *We can learn to do it better, as a human would!* Once we admit what is wrong.

Sometimes, when I consider history, I think that men and women, essentially, came to an understanding that men were lousy at sex and women just had to accept it. If so, that understanding has never worked for either gender. It just dug us deeper into our lunacy and created armed camps of the two genders. It is becoming more like a pressure cooker than a cauldron boiling over.

In the Buddhist belief system, Nirvana is the sad answer to Dukkha and Samsara. Like all other religious belief systems, it blindly accepts that this existence sucks and, then, you die. This preconception of inevitable misery is insane and, yet, unanimously accepted. That leads to defeat as a sentient race.

Nirvana is the removal of all attachments to this existence. The belief is that one can only reach the state of bliss known as nirvana by the complete cessation of one's existence which must be preceded by complete detachment from all that one could love in this life. So, their answer to the nastiness of living in this universe as a sentient being is not to do so. Leave all your loving behind. Just like western religions.

Wait until you die in order to avoid misery. Then, you can be happy??!?!?!? Woohoo!

I believe this is what always drove me on. I won't do away with what I cherish about life. I just want it to work right. I love so much about this life. It's just a damn shame we make such a shambles of it for no good reason. Force myself to love some awful human because that proves I know how to love? Let someone knock me around because that's the loving thing to do??!!? That's crazy. Love someone because they have attained their humanity? Now, that makes sense.

Maybe I misunderstand the intent of Nirvana. If it is the absence of all attachment to *worldly possessions*, I could get behind that.

Human or not

If you've read much of my previous work, you've probably noticed how much I despise the comment, "well, we're only human". It drives me crazy. The phrase should be "we're only a deranged animal" *and need not be*!!! Or, "Oh, if only we were human!"

We presume that because we were given wit and tremendous awareness, that alone makes us special. That there is nothing beyond our genes. We were given wit *in order to further understand this existence and ourselves*. We have failed miserably.

Welcome to the Theater Of The Absurd. The exit is right this way. Wit and awareness, alone, do not make us special ... until they are un-compromised and utilized.

All of the phrases that we use to hide our bewilderment are so transparent. "We're only human." "It's just a game." "Life sucks and, then, you die." "Life is pain." "Keep up appearances."

The natural order

I continue to ponder what other excuses we use to remain mired in the demented state of an animal. Upsetting 'the natural order' is one of utter stupidity.

It is not the natural order for a sentient being to hold on, in utter imbecility, to its animal characteristics, such as rutting.

It goes against life itself not to accept what our awareness made obvious and finally adjust one's behaviour through knowledge to accommodate the circumstances. That is what intelligence and awareness are all about.

Dimensions

Think of sentience as an extra dimension of the human animal. Sentience leads to the capacity to discern that there is more to sentient life than we have ever imagined.

Grand delusions

Every new generation is full of shit. Worse yet, revealing how deeply the delusions go, each new generation attempts to rebel and is finally brought in line by create their own bullshit that is even less relevant. The supposed conspiracy theories nowadays (even if they were true), as well as the pursuit to reveal them, does nothing to relieve the condition of our insanity. They just foment further distraction.

Bliss, not ignorance

For humanity, ignorance is not bliss. Ignorance is just remaining the witless animal steeped in a stupour while there is so much more that humanity can be. Humanity is not stupid but it is caught in a stupour. Only a very specific education will relieve the stupour.

Rise above

As a race, we are all about making things work. The critical anomaly is one instance in which we have bowed down to something for which there is no reason we should have ever bowed down at all. Instead of humanity making sex work, sex broke us. We threw up our hands in defeat. We cannot succeed at making sex something more than rutting? Our only aberrant options are to create perversions and little blue pills? There is nothing else on the horizon that can be directly interpreted as breaking humanity except for this one fiasco that we have avoided confronting. It's time for us to quit feeling broken and do something about it.

I like that I went the extra mile and found the answer to the problem. Even if I hadn't though, just realizing that we have fooled ourselves, creating our stupour, is a huge step.

It is crucial that we don't bow down to rutting in any way. The blue pill is just another form of rutting.

Skewed (or skewered) vision

It's pretty fascinating now, after the fact, to look back on the problem that mankind and each individual has faced regarding our dilemma. We are so preconditioned into a skewed version of reality from the moment we are born, that it was certain that it would take me a lifetime to first work through all of the bullshit and, then, finally, discern the source of our dilemma.

Everything a person reads, sees on TV, the web, or experiences through interactions with others causes a skewed version of the reality of sentient existence. This is true no matter what culture, society, or form of rule in which one is immersed. Only by looking past it all do we discover the underlying cause of our absurdity. That takes awhile

For me to initially see through all of this, it meant questioning everything regarding human life to finally stumble across the underlying cause. That's when the real work began - after three or four decades. The questioning of everything went into overdrive. It was a matter of battering down the walls of absurdity. Those walls are reinforced with nearly every expression and experience of a lifetime. I was able to step outside of it all and observe.

Sadly, that meant I never really participated in life - I had to become, almost purely, an observer rather than a participant. How could I become a serious participant when what I saw was so much less than what I could sense mankind could become?

I hope that my writings will make it much easier for others to break free and begin to set mankind on a course that is rational and loving. But, at least I have broken some ground.

Desperation

The ultimate absurd delusion is the desperate belief that each individual is responsible for their own sanity and nothing else. That we stand alone in our pursuit of sanity.

Humanity will never achieve sanity until we realise the sanity of our shared consciousness is critical. We must become interdependent as scary as that sounds to the beast.

We cannot shrug off those that seem insane and say it does not concern us. As much as we wish it were true, it is not a case of individual instances of insanity. If anything, they are like the canaries in the mine. They are symptoms that something is wrong.

Our sanity is dependent on the sanity of the species. Do your yoga, meditation, or Tai Chi, stoicism or cynicism all you please. Personal bliss or virtue, irrespective of the state of humanity, is not enough.

Everything else

Sorry to say, but everything else that humanity worries about from climate change to wars to domestic abuse to plagues to lunatic leaders and conspiracy theories just don't matter in and of themselves. They are not the problem. They are all surface issues. They will continue to occur until we resolve mankind's underlying problem. They are just the *results* of mankind's insanity. We will never rid ourselves of our insane actions and attitudes until we rid ourselves of the source of our insanity - if we last that long.

The burden

An interesting example of gaining our sanity will be that the urge to conscientiousness will no longer be a burden that has to be trained into each human. It will become the natural, accepted, shared responsibility of being human and sentient. I won't go further with this or, once again, I will feel the urge to tear my hair out and dive into some particular lunacies.

Sacrifice

For thousands of years, all the hopes and dreams of each individual have been reduced to ashes. No matter the success or lack thereof, most end their lives, at best, by saying, "well,

I did my best" ("I'm just human, after all" Aaarrrggghhh!) and/or "is that all there is to it??!?!?".

So, what is it about human life that leads to this nearly invariable conclusion? What crushes our dreams and hopes? There is that incessant something that is missing, something that begins to gnaw away *as we reach puberty*. It is a matter of *not* growing up. As a species, we have stayed doggedly demented, stunted, deluded, and childish.

It is a matter of the elephant in the room. It is the emperor with no clothes. We have been so preconditioned into nonsense that we accept sentience as a burden, a bane, instead of realizing it requires growth beyond just the intelligence and awareness with which we have been endowed in order to attain the vast potential of our sentience.

Second thoughts

As I review the books I have written on this subject, I have reevaluated my perspective. All of them, beginning with *Sentience* is dead on. It is just that they are the perspective attained at each step as my perceptions slowly cleared. The earlier the book the less easily accessible is the explanation. I certainly ranted a *lot* in the earlier books (except the chapter on Techniques and Considerations, which I have rewritten at least forty time for clarity). I have continued to strive to understand and explain the situation in finer detail, but they are all dead on. I leapt to the conclusion and skipped all of the intermediate steps in the earlier books while, also venting my frustration. The former is my natural habitat. It comes from being intuitive (see Malcom Gladwell's book on the subject). The latter was my relief valve.

Improvements

We sustain the perception that we have been improving. There are many so-called improvements that are very questionable. There has been little improvement of any consequence regarding mankind itself. Mostly, our material welfare has improved, not us.

The critical point here is the credulity of mankind. We want to pat ourselves on the back so desperately that we will dress up anything as an improvement and never look at the wide-ranging ramifications of even the simplest 'improvement'.

Desperado

You should now be able to answer the question asked in the song *Desperado* by the Eagles. If not, then you may have been listening to what I have said but you were not thinking.

Cavemen

I can just picture some caveman from long ago with just enough wit to realise that there should be something more to sex and, then, just shouting the thought down. After all, he was a MAN!!! He just needed to strut instead of think. Women were there to do his bidding! Why should he care if they also enjoyed the experience. If one got tiresome, just go club another one over the head. Instead, convince them that their part in sex is just making babies.

Then, again, I can picture the same man walking down 5th Avenue in an Armani suit with a briefcase instead of a club.

We really haven't changed much. Men have traded in their clubs (at least, in some cases) for power, money, or fame. We accept an animal's view of success.

A question that may never be answered is when did it become *consciously* apparent (to the race's consciousness) that there should be more to sex? Subconsciously, we've known it all along. I would guess that occurred over the last hundred years or so. A lot of women one or two generations ago never even considered sexual pleasure or, really, sex. Sex was just a necessary inconvenience to make babies.

Dragging the chain along

We wrap ourselves up in the same nonsense, superstitions, and absurdities of our ancient ancestors that cowered in caves. For all intents and purposes, all of the nonsense was developed by an unusually smart animal completely bewildered by a single difference from the other animals. Our antics remain chained, link by link, with each generation, to a burden that drags us back to our animal origins.

Wisdom of the ages

Calling any of our ancient antics "the wisdom of the ages" is a travesty. Calling it a disguise for bewilderment regarding the sentient state is more precise. We have idolized so much nonsense over the ages that it is no wonder that we have had a difficult time becoming human.

Our adoption of so much absurdity under the cover of wisdom touches very close to the heart of our problems. We *learned* deceit. We can unlearn it.

Wisdom of the aged

The same is true of the supposed wisdom of the aged. It is no wonder that the young of each generation rage and rebel against the views of the aged. While the aged have learned a lot about existence that youth has not encountered, no one has yet learned to become human. In our youth, we sense it. Until we break though, humanity remains a caricature.

All that we learn as we age is that nothing works the way it should. The one aspect of life that we were so sure would make it all worth it begins falls apart as we cross the threshold of puberty. Sex becomes less than the celebration of life that it should be.

Barriers to love

It is a mistake to believe that all it takes to love is the will to do so. It takes not only will but the use of some wit. And, of course, it takes two. A milk-toast version is the best that can be expected in the absence of sentient sex. Undiluted, fully sentient love is only possible when the barriers to our sentient perceptions have been eliminated.

Innocence

Innocence will not be something that is abandoned, treated as a flaw as we age, once we attain a human, sentient state. It is coexistent. It is integral to a sentient life.

Innocence is not wide-eyed, naive, gullible, witless acceptance as it is portrayed by a less than sentient race. It is the unaltered, undiluted acceptance of the human state of sentience and existence. It is undermined and misrepresented as long as we convince ourselves we are deranged animals.

Innocence doesn't stand a chance in the realm of an animal that has evolved past its origins and, yet, never attained a stable sentient state. In a sentient being, it is codependent on and compatible with sentient awareness. It is a feedback loop to that awareness. The current connotations distort its meaning beyond recognition.

Maybe, it is best described as a sentient perspective uncluttered by the animalistic viewpoint. The abandonment of innocence is due to the failure of the most essential tenets of a sentient existence: love, clarity, and self-respect. When they fail, innocence is, by necessity, lost.

In this particular case, I am talking about the broader definition of love. Not making love, but the resultant sentient attitude due to making love, the advanced form of sentient caring we call love. The fulfillment that can fill humanity once we become sentient ... and innocent. Winsomeness and love might even equate with sentience. Do not think that I mean that one should let someone bash them on the head in order to prove their innocence. That's just stupid.

Incongruity

I think I finally figured out what pisses me off so much lately. It is New Year's Day and I was thinking, "If it were just that I could write off the debacle that we call humanity, I could just exit stage right. Fuck this idiotic race!" But, there it is. I *know* we can do better!

At the time, while feeling so disgruntled about the stupidity of mankind after reading the headlines of the day, I was listening to music and it finally hit me. Everybody *knows* how fucked up mankind is*!* It's littered throughout the songs, headlines, movies, and conversations. It's everywhere!

Many songs express some of the consistent problems we encounter very well but we never get past the surface issues. The song that fired through was "That's the way I've always heard it should be" by Carly Simon which deals with the misery of relationships.

Creation of songs and poetry, in particular, can bypass the whole thought process and reveal the subconscious. There is a power and a liberation from self-deceit that can occur.

Why is it that no one can make the fucking leap to the point that lousy sex is the problem (or so few, actually, since Simone almost surely made the leap) and the failure is men's responsibility? Our blind conditioning is utterly frustrating.

Until we learn to do better than rutting like an animal, an animal we will remain. Sorry, (maybe) one last rant.

Relationships, again

I just can't decide how romantic relationships will work once we gain our self-respect, self-confidence. Relationships are just too close to the central issue to discern.

Once sex is completely openly discussed and heterosexual intercourse actually becomes fulfilling, maybe relationships will be seen to have more to do with compatibility in a sentient environment, including gender choice.

Will it be that the first person with whom one seriously engages will become the love of one's life? While that may seem far-fetched, I am not so sure. The other scenario, that is the usual case today, of a person meeting and engaging with many of the opposite sex seems the foregone conclusion with the only difference being that one will finally be able to settle down with one person for the rest of one's life (which is not the usual case today). Today, it is more like a revolving door.

Or, the whole idea of a single person being the love of one's life may completely disappear. This seems most unlikely but I'm not sure. Is the desire for one and only one due to the lack of self-worth, self-validation, and self-respect developed due to the overall lack of success at making love? Do we only seek someone else's approval in the form of love because we do not approve of ourselves?

Any of these scenarios seem possible and, maybe, it will end up being all of these scenarios (including those that prefer their own gender. I just wonder about missing that eye to eye sexual encounter) with the only outstanding difference from today being that staying with one person will not equate with misery and mundanity and any dissolution of a relationship will not require the often vituperative attitude towards the partner.

But, the huge difference that loving, fulfilling sex and abandoning the gap in our existence will create makes me think that the scenario of finding one person with whom to celebrate life seems most likely, however it is achieved. I guess I believe our existing sense of love is accurate.

Certainty and uncertainties

You know, the thing is that I'm scanning new horizons here. Due to that, there are only a few of which I am certain.

I am certain that, currently, a great many men are lousy at sex. Who knows how many, though 30% is certainly the lower limit. My own estimate of nearer 100% hasn't changed.

I am certain that if men become good at sex we will have drastically improved our situation and become much, much, much closer to being a fulfilled human, sentient race.

I am certain that all men can become good at sex. I am certain that it can become second nature for men once we flush the bizarre concepts that we currently retain.

I am certain that mankind does not need to be the absurd creature it portrays. I am certain that humanity can think.

The rest? I am trying to work it out but who really knows until mankind becomes human? How do relationships work once sex transcends what normally exists today? How long will it take us to shed our absurdity? How much of our destructive tendencies are eliminated?

There is one question that may never be answered. Could we have arrived at this conclusion at some earlier date in history? I'm beginning to believe not. *Desiderata.*

It's not magic

I always feel that one part of all of this is comprehending how such a fundamental change to our interactions will take place? It's not like everyone is going to wake up tomorrow and everyone is going to act human and sentient and loving.

It certainly will take some time to straighten out the mess we have made of sentience due to the continued brutalization of our existence for more than three thousand years.

One factor affecting the velocity of change will be the paradigms of nonsense we absorb as children. It is likely that those paradigms of nonsense only become well entrenched due to the disheartening feelings of confirmation that life is nothing but a mess as we reach puberty and attempt loving. As sex fails to be as fulfilling as we know it should be, the nonsense sticks. If so, things may change rapidly.

Inhabiting a base of honor, integrity, and self-respect is just the beginning. As that base becomes a commonality, the acceptance of delusion should rapidly fall by the wayside. The nonsense is so entangled in the way we approach everything regarding life, in the way we live and proceed through life, that unraveling it all must take some time. The rebellious desires of youth for resolution will help us along. Now that the youthful rebellion can finally have some teeth, maybe it can happen sooner than seems possible.

Like a human

As an example of finally putting the animal away, there is another difference we will find. Communicating like a human is radically different than the current doggerel. Communication is not about argument, contention, brinksmanship, threats, dramatic effect, or debate in order to win. Those are games of the animal. Communication is not finding ways to present nonsense as a convincing argument. It's not about scoring points. The farce of our current political debates makes me physically ill. "Vote" for whichever ilk you despise least. Yeah, right.

Reason

I can't hardly help myself. I just keep trying to dig deeper into this whole scenario of absurdity that we endure.

I am now driven to look into the next steps, because I am now rather certain that we won't even get started in any substantial way in my lifetime, which is utterly sad for me.

What is making me so despondent at this moment is that I see all of these critical insights starting to appear and, yet, the central premise that is so essential - that all men need (**_and can!_**) learn to be excellent at satisfying their mate is nowhere on the horizon. Women don't see any point in speculation and men are scared shitless that their "secret" will be discovered. There is an answer, dammit. Get on with it!

We wrap ourselves so tightly in delusion that I remain aghast. For instance, why do you think homosexuality is so popular (as well as other variations on the theme of sex)? Don't get me wrong, maybe some folks will always prefer sex with their own gender (or a particular person that just happens to be of the same gender). But, at least one *current* reason for the preference is some folks want to physically satisfy their partner and enjoy that loving engagement and *heterosexual* sex doesn't offer them that option. It is certainly distasteful for anyone to leave their mate unsatisfied or remain unsatisfied oneself. It is the reaction to that situation that currently defines much of our existence and our insanity.

Those that pursue alternatives to heterosexual sex are quite brave to pursue what is deemed unconventional (the nicest word to describe the vicious reactions by some) in order to provide loving physical engagement for both participants.

How many perceive the failed mutual sexual satisfaction and emotional fulfillment of heterosexual intercourse and, *then*, decided to go look elsewhere in order to fulfill the prospect? Until heterosexual intercourse is a consistently viable alternative, it is anyone's guess.

When a woman doesn't receive satisfaction or a man is convinced he can't provide satisfaction through sexual intercourse to someone of the opposite sex, then two alternatives are to find someone that can or some alternative way in which to make the situation work. These folks are quite impressive. They see through to what is missing. They so desperately desire to satisfy or be satisfied, that they will break the status quo in order to do so.

In the current environment, many heterosexuals are often violently opposed to homosexuality *because it makes them aware of the own failur*e at engaging in mutual sexual satisfaction. It is just more evidence that men are, by and large, lousy at sex. Someone that was receiving and providing good sex would not react so violently to others finding an alternative that provides satisfaction for both. Just another stupid division created that separates humanity.

Some just desire to love another physically, no matter the cultural rules and regulations, whether it be through the use of the tongue or switching teams.

Research

We grow up with great expectations for heterosexual intercourse that are seldom fulfilled. I feel like, besides the conditioning, there is an undercurrent that whispers, "Of course, men can't last. That's just the way sex works for us animals." And, we carry on in our forced stupour.

The flaw in any argument for ongoing failure is that we are not just an animal. We have the wit to overcome anything, *if we put our minds to it*. I am still amazed at just how easy it is for a man to last as long as necessary. How could we not have discovered this over the millennia? Some men must have figured it out. So, how did it not get passed on? Was it done without conscious awareness? Does the man just strut around thinking he's special rather than admitting that he discovered something? Did he hoard it?

There are plenty of research establishments purporting to study sex but they are just as hobbled as everyone else in thinking that men are lousy at sex and there's nothing to be done about it. They accept it as a starting point. *None* of the sex research establishments have really looked seriously at changing the situation. How ridiculous is that? With all of the researchers, scientists, and doctors studying the body, no one ever put two and two together? Incredible!

Heck, they can't even admit how prevalent the problem is. The wording of the studies reveal that every intent of all of those studies (by men) regarding men's performance has never been to uncover the truth but scuttle the whole question Well, I've covered this in enough detail in my other books. Suffice it to say that men's research, so far, is plain foolishness. Literally, a circle jerk.

Face to Face

Sometimes I wonder if folks make the mistake of thinking that I believe that face-to-face intercourse (insightfully and ironically, named the missionary position) or even that only heterosexual sex is acceptable. That is not the case. All that I'm really trying to say is that *good* heterosexual sex needs to be a viable option. Right now, good heterosexual intercourse is nearly non-existent for no good reason other than men don't know what the fuck they are doing and have never really even looked (double entendre). Even if some men can last long enough to satisfy a woman that is easily sexually satisfied, it is a struggle. Virtually no man seems to last as long as he pleases. So much for being done with ranting.

Unadulterated love

The more I ponder face to face intercourse, the more wondrous it becomes. It is like nature needed some deep seated wonder in order to awaken sentience. I am not stating bluntly that looking into another's eyes while engaging in the most intimate act is what caused something awaken in us. But, it is an interesting possibility. And, the failure certainly drove us crazy as we turned out the lights.

It is very easy to believe that the staggering fulfillment encountered by looking into another's eyes while filled with unadulterated love, will transform human life. No slightest tinge of remorse or disappointment would remain. Seeing utter bliss to be human fulfilled in the eyes of another would be transformative. It is life-affirming.

The converse is also true. What dejection, discomfort, disappointment, bitterness, and invalidation of life awakens when looking into the eyes of another as failure to fulfill the sexual contract of a sentient being occurs? It dumbfounds.

I still have some je ne sais quoi questions concerning the fulfillment of face to face sexual intercourse. It seems to imply much more than is readily apparent.

I haven't even begun to explore, in depth, the myriad facets of this particular aspect of loving, but I'm beginning to believe they may be more significance attached.

The chimes

As I scan the articles being written (mostly by women), lately, once again, I feel like someone must be hearing what I have to say ... and, yet, they are still missing the crucial point, if so. There are so many articles nowadays about women seldom achieving orgasm through heterosexual intercourse and why lesbians achieve orgasm so much more often. Still, the main, most important point, that men have something to learn regarding sexual intercourse is missing. We still just seem to accept it as unalterable fact. Until we admit what is really going on, it will become more and more like two armed camps. That is not good. We are waking further only to accept more unconditionally the disturbed state in which we exist.

We must move on to resolve the issue, not sidestep it.

Resistance

It reminds me of an experience I have encountered more than once. I walked into a feminist library, once, in hopes of finding someone with whom to discuss this situation. As I explained my views (not very well, I admit, as I was still struggling with the ideas), I was baffled to find resistance to the idea. It was as if they could not see past their long-held view that men were not trustworthy. I have also encountered this resistance when talking to other folks with other belief systems. The resistance always seems to come for some strongly held delusion that justifies our misery.

What it seems to come down to is that we really don't like those belief systems to be overturned. I guess that is why I fear that, without a detailed, definitive, thorough explanation, folks will shrug it off. My intuitive gesticulations were certainly not enough. It is why I continue to write.

Moving on

The strongest indicator that we have not gained our humanity, that we have not moved on beyond the animal, is that we still refer to the ways of animals as a guideline for human life. Such as, "Only the strong survive." Or, something I just heard that is so perfect as to blow me away: "Without the strong arm of the law, we are just animals.", which implies that we *are* just animals with nothing better than rules and restrictions to attempt to contain the beast. Maybe laws and other restrictions will still exist but their use should be, at least, toned down considerably.

It is because we have not attained a sentient state that those tendencies exist, not because we are descendants of animals. We have never accepted the difference that makes us a race that can transcend an animal's characteristics.

Derailed

We have been off the rails for so long that we can hardly see the track anymore. We were told long ago that love was important, not to mention its subsidiary components like honour, integrity, etc. We were told that more than once by more than one thought leader in the past. The problem is that no one ever tracked love back to its source. Love remains a vague concept with no justification for its existence because there was no understanding why it should exist.

It is like a split personality. The race clamors for love and simultaneously enacts a violent, clinically insane way of life.

Snapshot

I have explained humanity's problem in detail every way imaginable in these books but I can't help but be concerned that it's not getting through. That something else I could write would make it more easily acceptable, more easily understood. So, I continue to try.

It still staggers me that I discovered our problem. It wasn't like I was expecting to identify what is wrong with mankind. It just seemed the most interesting, consuming, important puzzle of our existence. And, it is just so obvious that there is something wrong. But, really, after thousands of years, how could anyone expect to find the resolution to our stupour?

Maybe I make things too complicated for most folks, so let's try this. Mankind is so ashamed of sex that we are secretive about it. Because we are secretive about it men can never ask anyone (or themselves) the question: how does one get good at sex? Therefore, a lot of men remain lousy at sex.

Gender characteristics

All of the peripheral delusions caused by the central delusion regarding sex are even more obvious, yet we never even notice them or we brush them off as just the way it is. The most obvious is the difference between men and women. We just accept that the polarizing characteristics of the two genders are the "natural" traits.

How wrong we have been. Women suggest the best that humanity can become. Men portray the beast from which we descended. It's that split personality, again, and it does not convey the gender characteristics of a sentient race.

The real characteristics should be complementary and are yet to be delineated. Let me just point out a characteristic that should exist. Men's discipline which will only come into being when men learn the discipline necessary to satisfy their lover. It is a trait that will transforms the human race, once it is sustained, and will, in some ways, define the male gender.

Men's discipline is currently almost non-existent. Men only play at being human. They bash their way through life only attempting to mimic sentience and hide their monumental failure. Can you even imagine the powerful affect of a male gender that is disciplined?

Note that this is a real defining difference between man and woman. For a woman, it takes no discipline at all to satisfy their lover. Their discipline is of another nature but, also, will be enhanced by an emotionally stable male gender. For a man, sentient sex takes a modicum of discipline which will become a basis of their characteristics. This emphasizes the crucial difference between men relying on some pill to mimic manhood and actually gaining their manhood. Men have always had the primary struggle to overcome in order for humanity to become sentient.

Femininity and humanity

There is a great deal of confusion between what is feminine and what is human. Some of the characteristics that are supposed to be feminine will be found to be general characteristics of a sentient race.

I am certain that a great deal of what is deemed to be feminine is none other than just plain sentient humanity. This confusion has instantiated many of our latest delusions. Grace, compassion, empathy, and gentleness come to mind. Commonalities and differences between the two *sentient* genders will need new comparisons to define what is truly feminine characteristics and what is just sentient and human.

Spin it

Let's try to perceive other aspects of the problem in an attempt to get a three hundred and sixty degree view of our current state and where we may go. This may also clarify a point regarding the validity of the source of our problems.

Intelligence can overcome a lot of the worst traits that men portray, of course. But, the traits of the animal still lurk in the background, even for the best of men. How can it be otherwise? A man may accept his emasculating failure intelligently (and not lash out) but, still, it lurks, haunting his humanity. As described throughout this book, overcoming bad sex unleashes other powerful traits of sentience, such as emotional stability and discipline.

No matter how you slice it, the lack hampers our fulfillment of the human state. It has to. It should be obvious that men should be able to do better at sex and that the violent tendency of the male gender is detrimental. That it is not obvious indicates the depths of our delusions.

The fact that very few will have ever thought that men can be better at sex gets to the heart of the problem. The problem, the most disturbing aspect of all of this is that men, and all of humanity, have been battered into believing that men cannot do better, so we just accept it, convince ourselves that we are no more than a smart, demented animal, and also accept the accompanying misery.

Subtle signs

There are so many signs of the disturbance that destroys our sentient state. I want to take a little time to note a few.

The games people play

Humanity has a bad habit of absurdity. We play so many games to avoid facing the truth. The biggest game of all is the blame game. We always, always want someone to blame. It is so common that we don't even question this behaviour. What is depressing is that the finger-pointing no longer has the slightest attachment to reality. No one even tries to justify their views with reason. Lunatic conspiracy theories are easier to accept than the truth. The paranoia induced by our delusions prevails.

If something blows up, blame it on somebody and move on to the next farce. This seems to be the next step in our idiocy. Our leaders, nowadays, stand before us with a straight face and lie through their teeth. It seems most people, in the past, would, at least, cringe a little. Maybe not.

The *side* of the argument is all that matters. If that leader is on your side, he is being diplomatic. If he is on the other side, he is filth. To me, they are all just liars.

It has always astonished me how our leaders are allowed to break so many rules of society and it is always justified by one side or the other. Why is it that no one can see the erosion of the species in all of this?

It's all a game

Even worse, of course, is the idea that life itself is just a game (existentialism or Theater of the Absurd). Nearly every philosophy is based on it. That is such a demeaning idea that it take my breath away and I can't delve any deeper into it.

Of course, there is also the game of the mating ritual. I won't get into that either.

Taking it further

I was just watching a pretty cool video on youtube - it was one of the 2020 songs of the year on a website. It was by one of the more popular female artists to arrive over the last few years. She was doing a lovely job of tearing into the worst of men's traits. Great song but, what a waste!

How much of our effort goes into lashing out? I'm not faulting the lashing out, so much. The woman's situation is horrible and they are finally attempting to address it. The fury they unleash on men is well deserved but get to the goddamned point! We just don't look deep enough. We'd rather play the blame game. We'd rather sink our teeth into the oblivion of misery rather than fix it.

It is men's issue to overcome. I have done the goddamned discovery for everyone, so all that is left to do is make it glaringly apparent and then, for *men* to make the change.

Make it happen! Men, themselves, are not the problem. Their unnecessary limitation and failure impedes us from fulfilling our humanity. ***And, it has no reason to continue!!!***

If someone doesn't feel comfortable with blatantly pointing out the truth, fine. Please feel free to point to this book to explain. Just say it is interesting and get the point out there. The chapter on Techniques and Considerations in *Sentience are* for those that are ready for the next step.

The most important thing, right now, is to make the predicament obvious and move on quickly to overcoming it. Women can do that just as well as men and have much more at stake, if you discount that all of humanity has its sanity and very existence at stake.

Domestic violence in all its varied forms from verbal to mental (errr, shouting versus mind games) to physical abuse, as well as its close cousins misogyny and sexism are just a few examples of the issues that make it pertinent to women to get men on track towards sentience.

These horrible outcomes are exemplified by the direct effect of the flaw in our sentient state that causes many of the surface issues that we complain about and play the blame game without any sane contemplation. Certainly, any sane mind can see the source of these issues ... and, yet, we don't. We are clinically insane.

More rules, regulations, guilt, etc are thrown on the fire to resolve nothing. We only secure the lid on the pressure cooker more tightly. As long as we continue to crash on the rocks of surface issues in howling fury, and never realise that there is a cause, we do not move forward. Errr, sorry, ranting and tearing my hair out, once again.

Patience

Okay, I've taken a deep breath and pelted myself, once again, to show a little patience, so let's see if I can explain the situation regarding broken relationships.

Beyond the paradigms and conditioning, there is also the camouflage of variance. In other words, using relationships as an example, many do not have bad breakups or, go through a lifetime with no relationship at all. This does not preclude these folks' destabilization, nor does it preclude their misery. Some people are just better at fooling themselves or attaining some measure of tranquility no matter how bad the situation gets. That is not the same as fulfillment.

A broken relationship will often bring the haunted feel that one has failed rather than awareness that it is the human condition that has failed. The feelings of failure, guilt, or anger grate against one's consciousness so that, when it all finally falls apart, it turns one's world upside down. *Especially* since no one is ever willing to admit what is really broken. From there, there are a variety of reactions. The blame game, of course, is prominent among them. Some one must be to blame, right? No one considers that the human condition is to blame.

Does the man become a miserable shell as it dawns on him that he is a failure and can't even blame a woman for leaving him? Or, is the man a dominant asshole, more closely mimicking an animal more than a human, that plays every game in the book to convince the woman that it is all her fault? Will he go so far as to enact physical violence, rather than the mental and verbal domestic abuse that is more common? Will he rack his brain to find some way to coddle or cudgel the woman into staying due to the subconscious feeling (that is never acknowledged) that her leaving reveals his sexual ineptness? The conscious perception of betrayal hides the subconscious sense of his failure. Is the woman even in a situation where she can walk away under such conditions? Does she have somewhere to go ... and feel safe?

So many relationships involve men begging for forgiveness. If one looks closely enough, what is it that he is begging for forgiveness from? Okay, I know how difficult it will be to follow that. I just hope that, if you have read this far, you can make the leap.

Yes, the same reactions can be seen from women but it is a rare woman that stands up for herself to such an extent. The example of moving into a shell is most likely for a woman.

Shrug

We shrug our collective shoulders at all of the idiocy of mankind as if it is to be expected. That is not to the expected reaction of a sane, rational, emotionally stable race of beings. It is expected of a race of beings that have not attained their sentience and, instead, settled for mimicking sentience.

The reason for unreason

We accept so many failed characteristics of humanity. Is it really reasonable to believe we are such a bunch of stumbling fools? There is an underlying deceit that whispers that we have failed as a species, so just accept it.

We have *not* failed. We have only accepted defeat in one most cataclysmic instance while it was not at all necessary.

The more I consider deceit, white lies excluded (or, at least questionable), I am rather certain it need not be part of our existence. It is the corruption of innocence.

I hope I have convinced you that innocence is not a bad thing. It is just poorly perceived. The connotations have almost ruined the word. Especially as the animal traits begin to take convincing precedence (existentialism prevails).

When our minds are freed to think with reason, innocence is looking at existence without delusion. It is staring into the face of existence without shirking. The whole human condition is currently based on shirking our sentience and, increasingly, making such innocence impossible.

So, what happens when the insidious failure that men have accepted is proved beyond a doubt to be only a failure to overcome? What happens when it is proven to be an unnecessary defeat for the whole human race?

The frog

I'm sure you all know the old saw about the frog in hot water. It finally dawned on me that humanity's situation is worse than that. Our sentience was born into the boiling water of lousy sex inherited from animals. The animals from which we descended have always been immersed in lousy sex. It is why we accepted it without a second thought.

Humanity does not feel the water getting hotter so, of course, we attempt to justify the condition.

Charade

We've even perverted the concept of love to suit the fictional script of our existence. Since the sex doesn't work as part of the answer in its current, inept form, we have substituted various confusing, inaccurate definitions of love as the answer to our dreams - that are never attained. It always remains a dream just out of reach for millennia.

Sentience and love are fulfilled by the act that we trained ourselves to consider shameful (even a curse by many) and take for granted that it can never be anything more than rutting. We look at sex and think animal, never contemplating that it must become human.

Even more preposterous, we place the burden of love on a thought process. Sex is just considered something we do because we are animals.

The glory of reciprocal, shared *physical* love never enters our minds. We just attempt to do our best to "love" someone without the physical fulfillment of love until it all falls part, as it inevitably does. Whether the relationship breaks apart or is tolerated for a lifetime, it rarely, if ever, ends with love sustained. At best, a shallow, distorted form of love remains.

I don't know whether to laugh or cry as I realise the vast expanse of our charade. The reorientation of mankind will be as straightforward as flipping a switch once we get our heads out of our asses.

Sanctity

Humanity's sentience is not improved by the efforts of the individual to achieve personal perfection of their *own* spirit, mind, or body. Sentience is not an individual, selfish effort to succeed at life, irregardless of the rest of humanity.

Rising above the insanity of mankind as an individual is a futile effort as long as humanity does not attain sentience. The sanctity of the individual cannot be fully achieved, by a sentient being, until the sanctity of the race is achieved.

The hammer and the anvil

I continue to attempt to understand the workings of our failure. One perspective reveals two parts. There is men's failure and there is the women's acceptance of the failure. It becomes even more bewildering as I delve deeper.

*Man*kind (the male gender, that is) never attained its sentient state. Due to the unacceptable failure, they remain befuddled by their ongoing attempts to avoid the issue and the lurking nature of the failure. Women attain their sentience with little trouble or fanfare. They are equipped for it. They *always* satisfy their lover.

But, this is where the whole situation becomes hazy. The situation had to grate. I can't begin to imagine the frustration. Maybe it is a matter of not really understanding what is going on with men. Maybe it was the initial acceptance of sex as nothing more than the necessity of existence and being an animal. It is possible that it originated in that deep well of their forgiveness and compassion that is a hallmark of their sentience. Did women never breach the issue at all until just lately? Did the fear of men's reaction become so deeply ingrained over the millennia that women learned it was better not to mention the failure at all?

In any event, men just continued to reinforce the befuddlement that was erected by their deeply befuddled ancient ancestors. Excuses continued to be laid on top of the original delusion and excuse. Confusion reigned.

Vibrancy

If you look around closely, it is easy to perceive the actual human condition that we endure for no good reason. Most people drone and drudge through life. The one's that don't are desperately grasping at life, play-acting out its celebration amidst the inhuman backdrop. Live for the day!

Human life is far from the vibrant experience it should be. What happens when we can provide a bold, confident face towards the future, replacing the sham of mindless blind arrogance that we currently feign in order to cover the cowering, uncertain, quavering beast beneath? What happens when we become human?

We are not approaching our humanity on our current trajectory. We are a yammering mess. Have you looked at the web lately? Especially, but not particularly, the news headlines, top stories, and attempts at blatant manipulation. There is a screw loose and completing the sexual ritual as humans is the only thing that can teach us love and humanity.

Youth and age

While it took me a lifetime of effort to understand what went wrong for mankind, the youngest are the most likely to be able to accept without hesitation and begin to fulfill. They are the ones that have not drowned in the delusions after years and years of failure. They can more easily reach the surface and take a fresh breath.

Love all

We proclaim phrases like "Love all" without any justification or ever acknowledging that, without justification, without a full understanding, it has never worked even though we have tried to do just that for at least two millennia.

It becomes an individual effort of will to 'love all', against the backdrop of the undermining influence and actions of the brute. Love is in conflict with the animal that remains to brutalize our existence. So, in the past, the suggestion was to love the brute, even as he bashes you over the head.

"Love all" is the natural result once we finally, decidedly, definitively differentiate the human. "Love all" will only only succeed once we overcome that which impedes our natural sentient instinct to love, once every human is deserving of the consideration.

The irony of love

One irony lies in the fact that we have known about love, in its broadest definition, with its subsidiary concepts (e.g.

self-respect, honour, integrity, etc) for thousands of years without ever achieving any of them to any significant extent. We make the attempt and it erodes away. That is true both as individuals and history. That alone should tell us that there is something missing. A common conclusion is that they are just high-minded ideals that have nothing to do with an animal's existence.

We bamboozle ourselves further and further, to avoid considering *any* human aspect in the metaphorical mirror. We are slowly learning that those characteristics are detrimental to success at life as an animal. It shows in almost everything we do and say. We are so far off the rails that we can't see the track. Those that shrug off the finer aspects of sentience and embrace the ruthlessness of an animal win within the context of an animal's existence.

That love is inherent and real is obvious because we see it in the innocence of children and most seldom lose the sense of love completely. It is shredded over a lifetime into smaller and smaller pieces as we lose the greater part of our sentient awareness and become more like just another animal and yet, still, hope for love remains.

Make no mistake, love does *not* need to be *developed* in a sentient race. It is *not* something that stubborn, dogged persistence will make real. Our inherent love and sentience becomes warped as we doggedly continue to avoid acknowledging the importance of sentient sex.

Love and sentience are always there just waiting to be fulfilled by fulfilling sentient sex. They are brutalized out of existence in a human being by the lies, disinformation, and misinterpretation of the beast that remain. All because we can't admit that men have not figured out how to keep it up.

We all hunger for love while desperately and witlessly avoiding the source of the fulfillment of love. We continue to commit to a storyline, initially created by an utterly witless beast, that obviates the fulfillment of love.

As we seek love, we inadvertently avoid the one and only aspect of it that can fulfill its potential. That is the utter irony.

Remaining human

There is probably another concern that will be voiced or, should, at least, be pondered. Humanity, so far, falls apart at a moment's notice when things go bad. We revert to the animal in a heartbeat. Why wouldn't that still be the case once we gain our sentience in full?

First of all, we have never, yet, departed the realm of the animal. We put on airs, attempt to act civilized, attempt to 'keep up appearances' until the chips are down. Then, the beast comes out in full measure.

That is the defining difference. We remain the gibbering beast without the fulfillment of love. We force ourselves to *act* human. We will finally *be* human.

Our sentient potential, once, established, will not fade like the facade that we currently maintain. Learning to physically love will become the expectation. It should become nearly instinctual. Once the breakthrough is accepted, the ease with which the man's proficiency is attained will make it a natural extension of being human.

Being human is a state of evolution. Just as the current state of the gibbering beast has been so difficult to throw off, the loving natural condition of a sentient being will be even more difficult. It is the natural state of a sentient being.

The beauty, rather than fiction

The more I think about early man the more I realise that it would have been impossible for him (as a gender-wide phenomenon) to overcome the difficulty inherent in bringing sex to a sentient level. The more I think about it the more I realise that it takes three components.

Beyond unshielding the heightened awareness that has been impeded by embarrassment (1), as well as the knowledge necessary to overcome the bewilderment (2), it takes a modicum of discipline (3) that early man (gender) would not have been able to achieve.

It needs to seep into the consciousness of the *race* (both genders) that a male human that has not acquired these three components in order to overcome the sentient sexual failure is not yet a man. He will remain in the quagmire of the animal until he does so. It is crucial to male maturity.

When we attain this state of consciousness, we will finally see all of the absurd male antics for exactly what they are and they will become jeeringly unacceptable traits.

While I become more certain every day that learning to make love, rather than just rutting, is our only exit from the Theater of the Absurd, I am beginning to think it is just that.

Exiting the theater of our current lunacy will allow us to begin to wander the streets of our sentience and discover so much more about being sentient. Learning to make love is just the starting point, the entrance to a sentient state.

It is not enough for us to be open about sex, though it is crucial to the discovery of our fulfilled sentient state. We *must* make the link between sex and love.

Throughout the rest of this book, I am going to attempt to explore what happens once we rid ourselves of that which has held us back, as well as how we might initially proceed. I am not certain that this part of the journey will be successful but I am hoping that it can at least lead later generations to explore our sentience further and accelerate the change, if necessary. I continue to try to make this extrapolation definitively.

In other words, I am going to explore the beauty of being human rather than continue the exhausting attempts to explain the fiction, delusions, disruptions, and deceit.

Ground rules and initiation

The more I consider, the more I wonder if there are some ground rules to the endeavor of achieving sentience. For instance, women ranting that men are lousy at sex will not get us there. It is reasonable and appropriate for them to rant about it but it's not enough. A few men achieving sentient sex is not enough. The blue pill is not enough.

The primary ground rule is that it needs to become unfailingly embedded in everyone's consciousness that all men must learn to perform sex as only as sentient being can and, thus, attain the sentient state of an emotionally balanced and stable, reasoned view of humanity and this universe and finally evolve beyond the animal.

Maybe a better perspective would be to ponder the initiation into our sentience. How do we get there? I've often said that every man desires to please his lover while engaging in intercourse. That is obvious. And, yet, it still happens seldom. That is the impetus that gets the ball rolling.

There are two missing elements. The understanding of how important it is for mankind to achieve loving sex and the belief (by men, especially) that it is possible. The desire by men to become successful lovers is certainly there. All that is really required is for men to accept that it is possible with reasonable effort. It is. It just needs to be accepted.

Before, in the previous books, I have suggested that it only happens as a ground swell, a grass roots effort that grows from the individual man. That is almost certainly the case. The quicker it becomes commonly accepted as possible, the quicker we become human. But, I am bit concerned that maybe there is more to it.

For instance, maybe, initially, until the surety of success reaches a tipping point, men will not desire to take the chance that they will look like a fool for trying (that ol' 'keeping up appearances' mentality). The fear and shame of failure (in my own experience) is rather overwhelming. Maybe I should only be addressing what is termed the lunatic fringe. Or, maybe, it is only the young that have not been fully immersed in the failure that will get it.

Maybe I'm just chasing ghosts, once again. Maybe it will just take more time. Forgive me if I'm impatient.

Once we open the door to the exit from the Theater of the Absurd, there will surely be the matter of the changes that we will face. Will it be effortless, serendipitous and copacetic? Just a smooth transition as we awake from the nightmare into our sentience? That seems very reasonable. We should expect that no one, even the most dyed-in-the-wool animal among us should feel threatened. It is not a coup or transfer of power. It will be only the slow, evolutionary evaporation of the desires of the animal. It will be a relief of tension, a release from the chain that runs back to our origins.

Still, it seems it might take a serious effort to unravel the many millennia of misdirection.

Honesty

Maybe the biggest burden that we assumed by hiding from our sentient state is our loss of honesty (innocence, if you like) as a crucial component of a sane existence.

Once again, I am treading on new ground that is difficult to explain. Honesty, I am beginning to believe, is a component of sentience that, once freed, can lead us to some rather striking and surprising results.

Serendipity

I have suggested before that there is something more to existence that we suspect. My own somewhat loose definition of serendipity seems as good a term as any to describe it. Love, in its infinite array and its subsidiary components (e.g. honour, integrity, etc), are something that we have stumbled over. In some ways, honesty seems directly linked to all of these components of a human, sentient life. Honesty seems bound up in the attainment of a sentient state and all of the components. How can one have honour, integrity, dignity, etc without self-honesty?

"A fortunate event or circumstance" is a good starting definition as any for the term 'serendipity', though it is only the starting place for my own definition. It is the term 'fortunate' that needs to be pondered in this exploration. 'Honest' may be more appropriate.

Throughout life, one makes choices on a moment by moment basis. In the presence of self-deceit, those choices are blurred by delusions that we developed. When the paradigms and conditioning mislead, the results may be worse than we think.

When one can make those choices from an honest perspective, the results may lead to some interesting horizons. If an undistorted lens of honesty is applied, the results may often seem 'fortunate'. In some ways, as I still struggle with redefining the term 'innocence'. Utter honesty, rather than naïveté or gullibility, seems a very good definition.

When everyone accepts their own self-worth, the changes may be more radical than expected. Acceptance of oneself leads to acceptance of existence as something other than a burden to be borne.

How to explain? This is more like a tickle at the back of my brain suggesting that there is more to it than we understand. How does one describe colours to a blind man? Until one has experienced it, it will remain a foreign concept.

We don't choose unequivocally. When the choices made are honest with oneself, will they lead to 'serendipitous' results? Wow, does that sound mystic!

I feel that somewhere, in the midst of honesty, resides more answers than we could possibly imagine. Still mystic! I state all of this hesitantly because it is just a feeling. We will need to get a lot closer to the reality before this can be explored much further.

Perspective

In order to begin the journey into what a sentient existence might entail, it seems that a deeper perspective on our current situation might be helpful. Once again, I am not so interested in answers as I am with the questions that seem never to have been posed. The breadth of questions is far more important than point or snap answers. It is only in a constellation of questions that we arrive at the right answer.

Rights of the animal

Freedom

There are so many terms glibly used that have never been very well-defined for me. Freedom is one such. Everyone desires 'freedom' but freedom from what? It is a vague concept unless you or your ancestors have been bound in chains as slaves. Wage slaves seem to approach the point. Slaves to our animal past seems even more to the point. Why is it that we all so desperately desire freedom? From what?

Is it the impact of our sentience remaining in chains? Is it the effects of our fettered sentience that leaves us feeling that we are all in chains? Do we desire freedom from the animal?

Privacy

Why is it that privacy is such a strong desire? What is it about our existence that makes us so desperate for privacy? It reminds me too much of the desire to turn out the lights.

Is it that we are embarrassed by something that we never want revealed?

Fear

This one is a little more clear. Why do we lock our doors at night, for instance? It is fear that some other human will enter our homes unsolicited. In other words, that someone will act like an animal. They may commit some crime against ourselves, our property, our family. So, maybe the real question is why is it that we fear other supposedly sentient creatures of the same race as ourselves? It is just accepted 'that's the way it is'. It is not enough to note that there have been crimes. It is the surety that we carry around that there will *always* be crimes that must be questioned. It is that boiling water, once again. This is a far more complicated subject. Someone in poverty, desperate to just stay alive is willing to break in. So, the question evolves.

We don't think very clearly about a lot of these situations. Or, at least, they have never been clear to me.

Traits of the animal

There are a number of conspicuous traits of the animal that are worth examining, as well. What will be the ramifications of shedding these lesser animal traits?

Anxiety

Even more than a common animal, we have a high level of anxiety that defines the race. Why is that?

Brutishness

I've mentioned this one often enough. We act like we are still a brute because we are. What will it be like to no longer be a brute species? We will be redefined as these characteristics become extinct.

Aggressiveness

Thoughtless, untempered aggressiveness is another trait that remains from the animal in large part. I feel like the obviousness of this condition explains itself. We are aggressive in our emotionally unstable state.

History rewritten

Another rather off-the-wall thought I've had in order to bring light on where we might head once sentience is attained is to explore the idea of a history in which we attained our sentience and learned to love at some earlier date in our existence. It's kind of reverse scenario planning. If we discovered the key about the same time, for instance, that we began to build cities, societies, and governments, and full scale war on each other, what would be different? What if we attained our sentience around the time that the industrial revolution and romanticism were struggling to define our existence?

War

Would wars have been avoidable? More exactly, would wars have never even been a consideration?

If one looks at the purposes of war, one really begins to wonder whether they could have been avoided by a truly sentient race. If every little distinguishable difference weren't defined by a state of paranoia and used to foment the masses, what would have been the results? Or, even more intriguing, if the ideas that we all hold so dearly that separate us never developed? Did our irrational paranoia create the need for bizarre beliefs? What if we did not cast those early thoughts of paranoid differences between people in stone like an anchor around our necks, drowning our existence?

Leaders

The previous thought leads directly to thinking about our desire for leaders. What would have happened if we did not have the desperate desire for someone to lead us? For a sentient race, would there really be a need for leaders? When I look at any leaders, today or in the past, I really question their necessity and, certainly, their value.

They tend to lead us into a snarling mess, such as wars. Yes, one can look at the likes of buffoons like Hitler and declare, "But, he was nuts! He had to be stopped!" Note, though, that he was just another leader that people *followed*. Is the whole desire for leaders nothing more than an animal instinct? Also, what led to his being so nuts? You know my answer. Is economics, the usual excuse for war, just a facade behind which lies our inability to attain sentient perspective?

I have contended for awhile that things will change radically when no one desires to be led or be a leader. The former seeming to be more important than the latter. In fact, the former leads to the latter. No desire to be led means no leaders. It was more just a sense until I started to realise that we were not yet sentient. Then, it became something to consider more seriously. No conclusions, just something to consider, a possible milestone of sentience.

It sounds like anarchy but realise that the most certain definition of anarchy is the lack of political authority or the state of society being freely constituted without authorities or a governing body or, maybe the best for tying into what I have been saying, a state of lawlessness.

Lawlessness, at first blush sounds bad, right? But, I've mentioned my thoughts about how most of the laws we endure are the to make us *seem* human, *act* human. They are there to constrain the animal. If we are, in actuality, human and sentient, is "lawlessness" really a bad thing or just the obvious result until we finally evolve into our sentient state?

I'm not saying it would happen overnight. They are evolutionary thoughts, not revolutionary thoughts.

Hierarchical structure and leaders

As I ponder leaders, I ponder the hierarchical organizational structure. It seems reminiscent of the animal. For beasts, this works just fine. The leader bites the backs of its followers until they do what the leader wants.

Is there the possibility that we could do just fine without organizing in a way that requires leaders? Can you imagine an organization in which there were no leaders? That everyone did valuable work instead of some telling others what to do and creating slideshows to justify their existence? A consensus approach, in which each person respected every other person's value and, at least, considered their insights (not something that happens often today), might do just fine.

I don't know how far I wish to go into this avenue of exploration. I could describe an organization in which everyone just did their jobs with some form of consensus about what needs to be done and how to do it. An organization in which everyone shared in the, values, results, and benefits equally. But, that may not be worth the effort. It is something that is far down the road of our sentient attainment, if it makes any sense at all.

I am certainly wallowing here in waters far beyond my depths, far beyond any definitive certainty. Just consider it wild speculation if that makes you feel better.

Industry

Here, I am not so much considering industry itself, though maybe I should. I am just pondering the way in which industry developed. The abandon with which we dove into producing 'stuff'. The abandon was surely driven as much by the mania to make lots of money by the few as it was for the desire for products, many that are of questionable value. There were many (and still are) that benefited hardly at all by the advent of the industrial revolution and many (including Earth) that suffer horrible consequences due to the abandon with which industry has been pursued.

The abandon with which we pursue so much is an interesting point. We rush forward with the least amount of consideration for consequences. I really have to believe this will change radically as we begin to acquire our sentience.

The finer qualities of humanity

The finer qualities of the sentient state are all based on self-respect. Self-respect enables self-confidence, self-worth, caring, compassion, empathy, generosity of spirit, honor, integrity, responsibility, grace, joy, decency, honesty, innocence, and the celebration of life in all of its aspects. And, probably a lot of other traits of which I haven't thought.

These finer qualities can only flourish in the absence of the the delusions that undermine self-respect and keeps us chained to the subservient animal mentality. Once the distortions begin to rampage through one's thoughts, all of the finer qualities are difficult to retain and extremely difficult to recover. Irrational ideas invade the thought processes and become deeply embedded and self-justified. There are no defenses against them without stabilization of the finer qualities. Rational, emotionally stable, critical thinking does not exist without them. How quickly our retained self-respect jettisons delusions will be a deciding factor indicating how quickly the human race can become fully human.

The dishonesty and overall corruption of the human spirit is absorbed from role models by osmosis while we are still too young to even consider the concepts thrust upon us. The firm hold of the lunacy depends on the destructive failure of sex as we reach puberty. The delusions remain questionable until the world is knocked cock-eyed at puberty.

Interestingly enough, it is easy to recognize the nonsense in someone else's belief system but not one's own. Another interesting note is that those concepts of nonsense become confirmed as we voice them aloud. That seems to make them more real. (I just realised this was one of the reasons I was able to avoid the trap of conditioning and paradigms, which led to this conclusion. In my rather bizarre childhood environment, I learned to remain silent because opening one's mouth always led to trouble. I never voiced the nonsense spouted by my parents or siblings simply because I never talked at all. As the years passed, I became an observer of life rather than a participant. That allowed me to develop a very different perspective on human interaction.)

How long will it take for the race to finally rid itself completely of our lack of respect for oneself as well as the whole of humanity? How long before sentient perspective becomes unchallenged by nonsense?

Phrasing the question as I just did may imply the answer. It really is such sheer nonsense that we tolerate. Since we can see it so easily in another's belief system, I would expect it will fade completely in relatively short order. The lies we tell ourselves must cause some degree of discomfort. Once we overcome our senseless fears, once the influence of puberty is no longer destabilizing, the delusional nonsense should become easily apparent - the nonsense that we are fed should become as unacceptable as the versions in others which we so readily recognize and deplore.

As the fear of the abyss fades, self-respect should quickly flourish. Unassailed by failure the finer qualities of humanity should reinforce themselves. At least, I hope so.

dual nature

Another piece of the puzzle finally falls into place for me - to some extent. Humanity's current condition is something akin to schizophrenia. Maybe it is due to the dual nature of the love and sex that we have not been willing to face. Maybe it is due to, well, being just plain driven crazy by our inability to fully inhabit our sentience.

The split between the conservatives and the liberals has always driven me mad. I have tended to always side with the liberals because of their tendency to attempt to appeal to our loving nature but, as I awoke today amidst the debacle (in so many ways) of coronavirus, I realised something further regarding our situation. It is that same confusion regarding love that causes that split personality. Some have been taught to love everyone, no matter how grievous their actions. Some are taught to withdraw from the world and love it from a distance. Some abide by these simplistic misinterpretations of love. Some are utterly repelled by them. All because we just have not understood the real intent of love or its source.

Love is *not* naive. A loving sentient nature is about compassion but also about seeing things as they are. It does not wallow in all of the nonsense that is put out there to justify the schisms that rock the world of humanity. Well, I don't want to get too into this. It could and probably will (at some point) fill a book (by someone other than me). The point I'm trying to make is that a sentient love is a discerning love. It's not about keeping up appearances.

Beyond the concrete

As I begin to ponder beyond the bounds of the nonsense we have endured while also pondering all that I believe I've learned, in an attempt to consider what the journey will entail once we abandon the bane of inept sex, I am struck by the preponderance of vague, poor definitions of love. We sing about it without end. We write and film stories about it in such volumes as to take one's breath away.

All of it has been like a blind man banging into tables and chairs seeking entrance into a new room, only to find himself sitting on the floor and making up fictional stories about the room he has never located, much less entered.

Love is more than we ever imagined or, more precisely, it is everything we ever sensed but could not fulfill, elucidate, or even describe to any great degree. That irony, once again, strikes me. The physical fulfillment of love was right there in front of us as we looked into the eyes of the one we loved ... but looked away, turned out the lights. Remarkable!

The heart and everything about a fulfilled sentient existence that makes it more than existentialism begins to clarify. It is about much more than just tempering the materialistic obsession of ours. It is about more than just exiting the Theater of the Absurd. That is only the beginning.

As I've mentioned, the simplest definition of love is an advanced form of caring only attainable by a sentient species. In many ways, it is as if the definition of sentience and loving are one and the same. Self-respect, honour, integrity, etc are components of sentience ... and love. They are liberated by making love, the most important advanced form of caring.

Only a fully sentient consciousness can reveal to itself that there is more to existence than the strictly materialistic perspective in which an animal exists. A sentient species *cannot* do that until it learns loving (i.e. make love, perform reciprocal loving, *share* physical pleasure). That push and pull of discovering this has been happening, oh so slowly, for all of our existence. Maybe the first tangible instance of it was some woman uttering the concept of love and, then, the concept of making love.

I realise the following sounds kinda mystic but I am just starting to feel like I understand to some extent, so bear with me. Mystic it is not. It has been baffling, just as everything was to those first animals that inadvertently gained a heightened awareness and intellect only to twitter it all away.

It is so darned astonishing as to take one's breath away. It is as if all of life, since the first amoeba, has been leading up to this. It is like the inexorable intent of nature (or the universe itself) is to be perceived wholly and in a way that astounds. Almost as if it desires to be relished for its awesome potential. Is there something beyond love that we haven't sensed? Probably.

I know that sounds mystic. Sorry about that. I have no better words. I don't think it's mystical as much as currently incomprehensible. It certainly remains a mystery to me.

In the sense of those words and phrases like love, making love, honour, integrity, compassion, etc. it is the culmination of so much that we have always sensed with our heightened awareness and pondered with our heightened intellect but, also, attempted to avoid like a bewildered, blundering beast.

As I shed more of the instability that our ancestors bequeathed us, the more easily I shed the absurdity that has burdened us all. That is still far from the goal of full comprehension of what it means to be human. I can just begin to distinguish the finer points of love and sentience as I peer past what obscures our view. I still feel blind.

It doesn't make it hurt any less that I spent a lifetime in the depths of the lack of that love. It is poignant and a great comfort, though, as I begin to comprehend the panorama of a loving sentient existence and the true meaning of love.

Those earliest expressions of love, like those sung in our youth, are the closest to the truth but still only a paltry expression of the full extent of love that a sentient race can eventually attain and evoke. That those expressions of love have been consistently dashed on the rocks of our aberrant reality makes me sad beyond belief. My only relief is the realization that it need not be that way.

Love revealed and, then, fulfilled

It may surprise you at first that I have written so many books (more than you will ever know) regarding this one subject. But, if you were to read through every one of them (not possible because my early explorations were never published as they were just my own maunderings and wanderings through our blundering existence), you would see the discovery process in progress.

It started long before I had anything worth saying as I was just exploring without any significantly definitive insights. It became serious with *Sentience* as I began to connect all of the dots. It began to fall in place with the realization of my own failure at sex, the most difficult to acknowledge and accept. The further, stunning realization was that I was certainly far from alone in that failure. That caused all of the tumblers to finally begin to fall in place. I was still far from being able to explain it at all well (four books, in fact).

Sentience was a self-examination of the ideas that finally began to hang together. *Sentience* was just taking the concepts out for a test drive. It was a method of verifying whether what I was considering made any sense when written out. My sense became more and more confident of what it had uncovered by putting the words on paper. Each book took it a little further and the confidence grew. It all hangs together now. I hope to goodness this book is clear enough.

I still feel I am hampered by a terrible inability to write prose. Or, maybe just that the subject matter is challenging.

In the past, there have been others that sensed the power of love but, while they could describe some of the aspects of love itself rather well, they did not delve into what impeded love as a sentient expression of life.

The difference in perspective between women that sense love best and men that hide from its failure caused a lot of the confusion. Sex became so taboo that it became like a curse to even mention it. The two genders became separated by a vast gulf of differing perspectives. The world is primed in every way for the unmentionable to be revealed and, thus, love, sentience, and sapience to begin fulfillment. A member of a sentient race (that's us) has always had this sense that hints that there is more to this existence than meets the eye.

I want to take a moment, in astonishment, to realise the panoply of characters that have worked to whittle away at this issue over the ages. On one front, there are those like Freud, Simone de Beauvoir, and the Flower Power Generation that have fought to open our eyes to the potential of sex. On the other hand, there are so many characters, like Martin Luther King, Buddha, Jesus Christ, and Ralph Waldo Emerson that fought to open our eyes to the potential of love. The intersection of the two brings it all into focus.

The sad part of this contemplation, for me, is the certainty that there is a long, long, long line of women that were intimately involved in this effort that will seldom gain even an honorable mention. They remained in the background in their loving way and let men take all the credit. Romanticism is just such an example. There is no doubt in my mind that women drove all of this. They have always had the best sentient perspective due to the reasons stated.

Beauty

All of the finer characteristics that comprise a sentient existence have always taken a beating. The saying, "in order to love others, love yourself first" is very true but, virtually impossible in the absence of physical reciprocal loving and the emergence of self-respect.

Another way that I like to consider love and the characteristics that are the outgrowths of love and self-respect is that they are beautiful. Both beauty and love seem only possible as expressions of a fully sentient being. As if love is an expression of beauty or, vice versa.

Love is not something that can be donned, like a raincoat. It is not something that can be pounded into the head of a beast. It is something that naturally flourishes and becomes self-sustaining. It is preceded by the fulfilling self-discipline of men in order for them to gain their self-respect.

Acts of Beauty

I like to think of acts of beauty as the loving expressions of a human, sentient being. Acts of beauty should become the commonplace expectation and definitive model for beauty. The beauty that mankind can portray once it awakens to its potential and bears the fruit of being truly sentient. Yeah, okay, I'm waxing poetic. Sorry about that.

I've been pondering how to go about seeking the first traces of that beauty of our undiminished sentient awareness. It seems the best way to get my mind off of the current imbecilic antics of the human race. A reasonable way may be to look for the beacons that indicate we are headed in the right direction, like a form of scenario planning.

There will be some early indicators that we are gaining ground on becoming human as we learn the self-discipline that leads to self-respect and, thereby, release our emotional stability, love, reason, dignity, honour, etc and sentience.

The increasing prevalence of acts of beauty will be first.

Beacons

The first beacon that came immediately to mind is that people will begin to care about others at least as much as themselves. Under all of the platitudes and promises, the real underlying view today is vociferously stated as "Take care of number one first." It is the current mantra that is seen but seldom stated because, under it all, most of us remain human to some extent and attempt to *act* the part. In actuality, many take that statement beyond to convey "take care of number one to the exclusion of all others." Token efforts to the contrary are all that exist of love, beauty, and sentience.

It will be obvious when mankind cares about humanity as a whole as much or more than oneself. When the success of the whole of humanity and each individual overrides the rationalizations of self-interest we will be well on our way but that will be a late, rather than an early, indicator.

The change mentioned above sounds a lot like like the Golden Rule: treat others as you would like them to treat you. The only real difference being that, while the rule makes sense, the force implied by having to state it at all, does not. Learning it intellectually is close to useless. Our history proves that. Most concepts of right and wrong have deteriorate to the degree of whether it is legal or not. One need only find a way around the law. The comment now is, "It's legal!", no matter how despicable it is.

So, maybe that is another, more subtle sign for which to look. When many rules, laws, and regulations begin to seem superfluous. Maybe when jails begin to empty rather than fill.

There is a more general beacon to seek. When mankind begins to become beautiful, seek beauty, and create beauty. I'm probably getting too poetic, again. Sorry about that.

Maybe the very first indication that things are changing is when humanity begins to look forward with high expectations. Hmmm, maybe when headlines begin to move away from occasions for armchair rubber-necking?

Validation

I asked a question at the beginning of this book. How different would humanity's existence be if every individual human felt inherently validated in its existence? Do you see the point of the question now? Do you see its intent? Do you see its relevancy?

I look around and see all of humanity struggling to prove their worth in aberrant ways. Almost exclusively, we *only* pursue success in the material realm. We give up on anything else early enough in life.

The way in which we attempt to prove our worth is utterly insane. This leads to all of our problems. In general, most do not care about the ramifications of their choices, actions, and viewpoints on humanity's existence. Each is just too self-involved in desperately attempting to (erroneously) validate their own existence. The intent is only to validate one's *own* existence, prove one's *own* worth. It is a considerably insane part of our condition. Any ramifications, other than one's own welfare, play an almost non-existent part in our antics.

What if every human felt naturally validated in their own existence without all of the claptrap? What if questionable pursuits were questioned for their actual value rather than their profit?   So many of our pursuits are dominated by the desire for profit, irregardless of the affects on humanity. Long term effects are mostly out of the question. That is the view of an animal that doesn't care what happens beyond their own lifetime. What if the inherent value of a pursuit was more important than profit or whether one gained attention, influenced masses or, in some other way accrued recognition and aberrant validation?   What if the fifteen minutes of fame was acknowledged as a foolish desire?

This will be a major portent that we are really getting our existence on track as a human, sentient race.

And, now, I fully understand my desire for anonymity.

Blazing trails

As long as humanity is inundated with the nonsense that we accept in our youth, we will be at the mercy of that nonsense. Once all of the nonsense is accepted as nonsense, we can begin to blaze new trails into sentience.

The first step is to recover the nail and hammer it home.

Once a generation has been born that does not bear the slightest remnant of those embedded delusions, once the previous generation no longer passes those thoughts along to their pre-pubescent, pre-critical thinking children as fact, the stage will be set to become human and sentient. I can't think of a more thrilling expectation.

Burdens and behaviour

The unanswered questions that remain regard the details of our future scenario. I am fairly certain I will have little more success other than to, maybe, outline the situation and ask a few question that might be indicative. It will, more than likely, take a mind that has not spent a lifetime battered by the absurdity and superstitions of our current predicament in order to get much further than that.

Bewilderment

In retrospect, the most shocking realization has been that we *didn't* see the sex conundrum. How could we possibly have bewildered ourselves to that extent?   We have so severely blocked out the fact of the missing nail that we act as if it doesn't exist, even though it is the direct cause of so many of our ills and the indirect cause of most, if not all, of the rest. We just swept it under the rug and entirely ignored it. Bewilderment was, thus, allowed to seep into everything human. It binds us to the animal context that we still retain. The door of bewilderment has been left wide open for all of the other absurdities that we accept in our lives. It is so utterly witless that it leaves one breathless to contemplate.

What happens once we become a race that is no longer bewildered? What happens once we stand confident, knowing what is really going on? What happens once we stand confident, knowing that it no longer needs to be that way ever again? What happens once the missing nail is fully recovered? Will the reorientation of mankind be as straightforward as flipping a switch?

These are not small questions. Maybe, you can begin to see just how it impacts our lives and the tremendous change that we should expect once we are no longer prone to bewilderment. Just as we are gaining our critical thinking, puberty comes along to wipe out any hope for rational thought. By the time we reach puberty, we should be well on our way to maturity. Instead, maturity is derailed forevermore.

Force

One of our most commonly accepted practices that will be difficult to believe we can change will be our desire to force *everything*. We so accept force and enforcement as the only way in which to get people to enact acceptable behaviour that we cannot imagine a world in which it is not required. The term *brute* force rings so true. There is zero belief that people can do what's right without being forced to do so. There is nearly zero belief that people will apply effort to life without a material incentive. That desire to force the issue, as well as the need for a carrot, are apparent in everything we do. That is the impetus that our desire to force *all* of existence to fit our desires without the slightest thought of just how stupid that is. A more subtle factor is that men desire to control everything because the have not learned to control the one thing that counts.

As we enter the 3rd Millennium, many of the traditional forces that we have relied on as demented animals in order to mimic being civilized are beginning to break down. Our sentient awareness struggles to be released from the drivel of our past. Nature itself even seems fed up. The absurdity is becoming clearly apparent which is only driving us further insane. It may be the most dangerous situation we have ever faced. We are looking into the depths of the abyss with solid belief in its inevitability.

Our intelligence and awareness are becoming more destructive as our sentient qualities remain elusive and, in fact, atrophy.

The carrot

The perceived need for the carrot is very intriguing. It is Pavlov's dog all over the place. And, we accept it because our witless non-sentient state, in other words the animal, responds to it. It's enough to make me sick.

There is a deeply embedded belief that humans only stir themselves to effort for the sake of a payoff. The most blatant example of this is, of course, money. We are all *forced* into efforts for the sake of remuneration as if we have no desire to create, produce, or otherwise participate unless we are rewarded. It plays to the witlessness of Pavlov's dog. We are not a dog, even though that is becoming the accepted conclusion. We have to fulfill the sentient state in order to become more than a witless animal. Currently, those that treat humanity as a witless dog are celebrated for their success. And, I feel sick, again.

We are so mixed up that we deem this as human. This is only the beast that we have never overcome. We have not attained the human state, thus do not respond to human standards. It never crosses our minds that the fulfillment - in the form of creation or contribution - is enough of a reward for a fully sentient human.

I could go much further but it would prejudice the case. I'll leave it for later generations to extrapolate, generations that can view the current disturbance as the history of our evolution without ingrained bias and delusions. Generations that will easily extrapolate from the sanctuary of a loving existence. The necessary fully transformed perspective, at this point in time, seems unattainable. For a race steeped in sentience, it will be as clear as space with no desire to rant.

Fiction

The best word to describe our current existence may be "fictional". Everything has been built upon the lie that everything is alright. That is a fiction. The unspoken expectation is that we will never be alright.

This all leads to the suggestion that maybe the best phrase to describe our situation is utter confusion (or, idiocy, once you begin to see the truth of our predicament). It is a web of confusion and fictional accounts that no one has looked beyond. What's left of our intellect is only applied to surface issues in order to keep up appearances that we are doing something pertinent.

As humanity looks back on its existence, after discovering its sentience, it will be astonished to find just how duped humanity was. From the supposedly non-fiction accounts of history to the day-to-day accounts of existence to, most blatantly, the fictional entertainment that sustains the illusion. At the heart of it all is the undeniably lousy sex from which we desperately desire to hide.

Panorama

Think

The most important milestone is when humanity, unfettered from the lies, finally, really begins to think honestly. As emotions become stable (not non-existent) and delusions wane, it is almost certain that thinking will become clear and truly successful for the first time in human history.

Retrospect

It will be an interesting time to live as mankind wakes up to the truth of its past existence and realises the fictions we have endured. The closest I come to the visualization is the analogy of a magic trick, sleight of hand, or con job.

It is shocking to realise that we have been living a fiction for thousands of years, each little brick of nonsense and absurdity further reinforcing the totally fictional account of our existence, while the whisper of our humanity continues to haunt us. The concepts of love, integrity, dignity, honour, etc are just sounds that we sense but cannot fully comprehend.

Turning a phrase

Let's try a different approach. Maybe that will open new avenues to our understanding. It may just be a matter of being picky about terms and phrases but, if there is one thing I've learned from all of this, it is that we are terribly sloppy in conveying what we mean and that is important to understand.

The saying goes, "one must love oneself first in order to be able to love another". Maybe a better way to put it is that "one must respect oneself in order to open up enough to love oneself or another". The lack of self-respect leaves a man barren of the ability to express his love because he senses it is a lie while he cannot fulfill the woman sexually.

More questions

What happens when the most intense experience of being human is followed by disappointment (note that both genders suffer disappointment if the reciprocal loving is not fulfilled)? How big will the difference be for humanity when the experience is commonly fulfilled?

What happens when we begin to trust ourselves as individuals, then, as a race? How transformative is it when we no longer need to introduce fiction into our lives in order to survive?

It comes as quite a surprise to realise that what we describe as matured should be replaced with the terms brutalized, deluded, and conditioned to remain in an animal state. What happens when we really mature? What happens when innocence, bolstered by understanding, proceeds throughout a lifetime? What happens when innocence is no longer a dirty word that has been misunderstood? What happens when offensive behaviour is not instigated by failure and, thus, nonexistent? The only current guiding light into all of these questions, as dimmed as it may be, is women.

The three dimensional puzzle

This journey of solving the riddle of mankind's lunacy so that we can fulfill our sentient state continues to amaze me. I had been mesmerized by the fact that we rut like animals, only to find it to be the smallest part of the puzzle. Crucial to understanding the whole picture but so small in the context of a fulfilled sentience. It really is all about humanity gaining the momentum of its sentience in full.

As I mention at the very beginning of *The cornerstone* and this book, it is about humanity gaining those aspects of human life that are contained in words like honour, integrity, empathy, and compassion in full. It has to become second nature for humanity. It is part and parcel of being human. It will be another indicator that we are fulfilling our sentience. It will open doors not readily apparent today.

Lexicon

The most subtle change may be a change to our lexicon, the use of words and the way they are used. This, more than anything else, describes best the depth to which our conditioning exists. It is littered throughout our written works and the very words and contexts we use.

A specific example. I'm not sure that the word "opponent" will have any real meaning in a society of humanity rather than a beast. You may scoff at that. We'll see.

Transcendency

I guess that which I'm leading up to is, as a constantly renewed view convinces me of the depths of our current depravity, I am much more convinced that the transformation we are facing is more staggering and transcendent than anyone can possibly imagine at this time, more transcendent than most anyone will be willing to accept at this time.

Groundswell

Another point that I have reiterated is the change will be a grassroots effort. It will be mostly ignored by those that strut on the stage of the Theater of the Absurd for all to see.

By necessity, it will be an organic change (though I hate that term immensely for its inconsistency). There is no need for ranting and raving in order to produce the change. That may seem an ironic thing for me to say, since I have ranted and raved so much about liberals, conservatives, exorbitant wealth, and leaders. The change will, by its very nature, relieve the desire to rant and rave.

Transition

This seems to lead well into a further description of milestones or beacons depicting the scenario of humanity gaining its humanity. It seems likely that, rather than the overthrow of our current institutions, they will change from within. As folks gain their self-respect and other sentient qualities, the quality of the institutions will also improve.

I'm sure, somewhere or other, I've mentioned how populations of people (whether an institution, organization, culture, or other structure or subcategory containing multiple humans right up through the human race itself) can be viewed as an individual. While it is made up of more than one human, it still expresses itself as a human in its thought processes, emotional make-up, and other qualities.

As such, they will change as the individual humans change, by gaining its self-respect and other human qualities. So, I am thinking, that very, very little of the structure of our existence will, at least initially, change regarding how humanity is organized and expresses its will. It is just that the quality will becomes more human in its expression.

We say that the 'machine' is in charge. Who populates the 'machine'? What are the working parts of the machine? A group of unstable humans. Look even closer. What gender is mostly in charge of the 'machine'?

When reason reigns

If you think about it, reason doesn't stand a chance in the Theater of the Absurd. In fact, it is predefined as impossible by the very perspective of existentialism. In our current setup, the obnoxious unreason of an animal always has the upper hand, since it is willing to lie, cheat, steal, even kill to get its way. Reason is dealt a killing blow by the deceit, delusion, distractions, and bewilderment created by the obnoxious habit of rutting like an animal.

So, what happens when obnoxious unreason is no longer viable? What happens when loudmouth morons are no longer acceptable? What happens when the accepted rules of a society, like not cheating or beating on one's wife, are actually followed - and, even further, when the rules are not even required?

What happens when reason reigns? It will definitely be a case of "if you can't beat them, join them". Or, "Omigoodness, I can actually be human instead of this despicable heap of refuse."

Transformation

The general question that still remains is what form will the transformation take? Will it be a slow, painstaking process that takes longer than three generations or, as I tend to believe, take place, in large part, within three generations from its beginning point? The beginning point, the pebble that starts the avalanche is obvious because there is only one that can begin the change: men begin to accept that they can make love in significant enough numbers to make a difference and pass it on to their male offspring.

Many, in the first generation, will require instruction. I am not concerned that those instructions will tail off, once the momentum is achieved. That is one of the key points. The instruction will just evolve past the need for the book *Sentience* as fathers become confident.

Fathers, today, have no desire to have that conversation about how to make love because they have no answers. A father that finally understands how to make love will rejoice in passing it on to his son. He will actually have something worth saying! Finally! Can you imagine the change that this simple step will produce?

The need for that conversation may even tails off as the knowledge becomes instinctive. That may take centuries and may be the final beacon that we have reached our sentience in full.

So, back to the primary question that I am unable to answer. How long will it take to fulfill our sentience? I think it is a question worth asking for every generation to come until the day that we finally can look in the mirror and say, "Yes, we are there." The question itself creates momentum.

Ending the cycle

Throughout my books you should be able to see how I have progressed. Initially, I was frustrated and furious to be put in the position to reveal mankind's sanity. The fury was part of the process of exorcism of the absurdities that were laid upon me in my formative years. The frustration was that I had to spend a lifetime figuring out what was wrong rather than living and loving as a human because no one else had taken the time to figure it out before me.

Excuse all of my ranting and venting. I was raised in an offensive, righteous household that took most of my lifetime to shed like a poisonous skin that attempted to corrode my soul. It seems some of the damage done, like a broken bone set incorrectly, will never heal completely. One can work on it for a lifetime and minimize its effect but its effect never, ever goes away completely.

I point this out for a number of reasons. One reason is that it just feels good to look the beast straight in the eye one last time and say, "Fuck you!!" The second reason is that it emphasizes what I have been saying. Even as a person sheds the nonsense of the beast, the marks of its claws remain throughout a lifetime. Better luck to the coming generations of humans in never encountering the claws of the beast.

As I review history, recent and ancient, I think, once again, of the poem, *Desiderata*. I have so often wondered if maybe this should have or could have happened in the past. I am now convinced that, no, it really didn't make sense at any earlier point in history. I still think that the time of struggle between the industrial revolution and romanticism might have been a better era for the fulfillment of our sentient state. I think we have drifted very far from a sane state since. But, the culmination of love seems destined to happen only after certain events preceded.

The end

I end this book as I should have ended all the others and, in fact (if not in print), did end all of the others. I hope to goodness that I have finally gotten through to humanity to the extent that I hear the answer echoed back to me. I am very, very tired of writing and the results of our transformation do not change, not matter how much I write. They just need to get started. I really don't think that another book will help. It's all stated pretty clearly here. My only fear is that my prose is not as impelling, enthralling as it might be.

Let me just say that, while I was the one able to penetrate the veil of all of the nonsense we endure, I am not sure I am the best person to convey it. I surely hope that someone, though, will now be able to see through all of the bullshit and convey the situation in a much more palatable form, if this doesn't suffice.

The animal and the divine

Is humanity an animal or divine? Humanity is the animal that can become divine through the simple expediency of accepting the difference that makes it sentient and, thus, remove its shackles to the beast.

Garden of Eden, revised

We have never laid eyes on the Garden of Eden, much less set foot in it.

When mankind first emerged, it was into a thrashing environment of kill or be killed and we were no different. Any other proposal is so ludicrous as to be offensive.

Now, finally, we are on the doorsteps of the Garden of Eden. Even if only a handful of people begin paying attention, we will get there. It will be an existence in which humanity finally learns how to exist as a sentient being in relative harmony with existence. Mostly that means in relative harmony with humanity itself. We will finally be comfortable with the thought of being human.

whickwithy@gmail.com